FAST FOCUS

A QUICK-START GUIDE TO MASTERING YOUR
ATTENTION, IGNORING DISTRACTIONS, AND
GETTING MORE DONE IN LESS TIME!

DAMON ZAHARIADES

ARTOFPRODUCTIVITY.COM

CONTENTS

Other Books By Damon Zahariades   vii

Your Free Gift   1
Wise Words From John D. Rockefeller   3
Foreword   5
What You'll Learn In Fast Focus   9
How To Squeeze Maximum Value From Fast   12
Focus

PART I
LAYING THE GROUNDWORK

Focus Defined!   17
Why We Lose Focus   21
Top 10 Obstacles To Staying Focused   25
7 Ways Improved Focus Will Positively Affect   31
Your Life
Pop Quiz: Do You Truly Have A Focus Problem?   35

PART II
**HOW TO CREATE AN ENVIRONMENT THAT
HELPS YOU TO FOCUS**

Lighting   41
Background Noise   43
Comfort   46
Ambient Temperature   49
Air Quality   52
Scents   54
Presence Of Others   57
Organization   59
Clutter   62
Time Indicator   65
Dry Erase Board   68

PART III
23 TACTICS THAT WILL IMMEDIATELY IMPROVE YOUR FOCUS

Tactic #1: Set A Timer   73
Tactic #2: Limit The Number Of Daily Tasks   76
To Five
Tactic #3: Know Your Reason   78
Tactic #4: Begin Each Work/Study Session With   80
Aerobic Exercise
Tactic #5: Capture Ideas Quickly   82
Tactic #6: Identify Triggers That Lead You To   85
Distraction
Tactic #7: Use A Daily To-Do List   88
Tactic #8: Play Music That Helps You To Enter A   91
Flow State
Tactic #9: Take Frequent Breaks   94
Tactic #10: Take Short Walks   97
Tactic #11: Commit To Single-Tasking   99
Tactic #12: Batch Process Similar Tasks   102
Tactic #13: Arrange Your Day Into Time Chunks   105
Tactic #14: Disconnect   108
Tactic #15: Limit The Time You Spend In Meetings   110
Tactic #16: Reset Others' Expectations   113
Tactic #17: Turn Your Phone Off   116
Tactic #18: Manage Your Energy Levels   119
Tactic #19: Meditate   122
Tactic #20: Avoid Your Email   124
Tactic #21: Create (And Stick To) A Daily Routine   127
Tactic #22: Tame Your Inner Perfectionist   131
Tactic #23: Reduce Your Caffeine Intake   134

PART IV
BONUS MATERIAL: HOW TO FOCUS WHEN WORKING IN COFFEE SHOPS

Face The Wall   139
Ignore The Door   141
Wear Headphones (Or Earbuds)   143
Listen To Instrumental Music On A Loop   145
Train Others To Not Interrupt You   147

Final Thoughts On Developing Fast Focus   149
Did You Enjoy Reading Fast Focus?   150

About the Author   153
Other Books By Damon Zahariades   155

OTHER BOOKS BY DAMON ZAHARIADES

The Mental Toughness Handbook

The definitive, step-by-step guide to developing mental toughness! Exercises included!

To-Do List Formula

Finally! Discover how to create to-do lists that work!

The Art Of Saying NO

Are you fed up with people taking you for granted? Learn how to set boundaries, stand your ground, and inspire others' respect in the process!

The Procrastination Cure

Discover how to take quick action, make fast decisions, and finally overcome your inner procrastinator!

How to Make Better Decisions

Here's how to overcome indecision, make smart choices, and create a rewarding life in the process!

The 30-Day Productivity Plan

Need a daily action plan to boost your productivity? This 30-day guide is the solution to your time management woes!

The 30-Day Productivity Plan - VOLUME II

30 MORE bad habits that are sabotaging your time management - and

how to overcome them one day at a time!

The Time Chunking Method

It's one of the most popular time management strategies used today.
Triple your productivity with this easy 10-step system.

80/20 Your Life!

Achieve more, create more, and enjoy more success. How to get more
done with less effort and change your life in the process!

Small Habits Revolution

Change your habits to transform your life. Use this simple, effective
strategy for adopting any new habit you desire!

Morning Makeover

Imagine waking up excited, energized, and full of self-confidence.
Here's how to create morning routines that lead to explosive success!

The Joy Of Imperfection

Finally beat perfectionism, silence your inner critic, and overcome your
fear of failure!

The P.R.I.M.E.R. Goal Setting Method

An elegant 6-step system for achieving extraordinary results in every
area of your life!

Digital Detox

Disconnect to reconnect. Discover how to unplug and enjoy a more
mindful, meaningful, and rewarding life!

For a complete list, please visit

http://artofproductivity.com/my-books/

YOUR FREE GIFT

∾

I have a gift for you. It won't cost you a dime. It's a 40-page PDF guide titled *Catapult Your Productivity! The Top 10 Habits You Must Develop To Get More Things Done.* It's short enough to read quickly, but meaty enough to offer actionable advice that can change your life.

I'd like you to have a copy with my compliments.

Claim your copy of *Catapult Your Productivity* by clicking the link below and joining my mailing list:

http://artofproductivity.com/free-gift/

Before we dive into *Fast Focus*, thanks are in order. I'd like to thank YOU. Many books promise to help you master your attention and ignore distractions. You've chosen to read mine. For that, I'm grateful and honored.

On that note, let's roll up our sleeves and get our hands dirty with material that's going to change the way you work. And in doing so, I'm confident it'll greatly improve your ability to get important work done in less time.

You're going to *love* what's coming your way in the following pages.

WISE WORDS FROM JOHN D. ROCKEFELLER

"Do not many of us who fail to achieve big things... fail because we lack concentration — the art of concentrating the mind on the thing to be done at the proper time and to the exclusion of everything else?"

- John D. Rockefeller

FOREWORD

~

Phone calls, texts, email, Facebook updates, Twitter tweets, new Pinterest pins, Instagram pics, news and gossip websites... the number of distractions that threaten to destroy our focus is growing. It's no wonder so many people complain that they can't get enough done.

Think about *your* typical day. Are your thoughts often scattered? Do you have difficulty concentrating on the task at hand? Do the slightest disturbances pull at your attention? If so, you're experiencing a common problem, one that affects millions of people: inadequate focus.

The good news is that there's a simple solution. All you need is a *system* for developing and strengthening your ability to concentrate. *Fast Focus* gives you that system in a simple-to-read, easy-to-execute format.

This book is written for you if you who struggle with any of the following issues:

- You can't seem to get things done in a timely manner. You miss deadlines and your productivity plummets.
- You tend to put things off. You postpone important tasks, choosing instead to spend your limited time responding to texts, surfing Facebook, and reading news websites.
- You're easily distracted. A single text or email pulls your attention away from whatever you're working on, and demolishes your momentum in the process.
- You're prone to daydreaming. You find yourself staring off into space, entertaining one or more fantasies when you should be working on the task in front of you.

Can you relate to any of the above challenges? If so, you're in good company. They affect millions of people, including straight-A students, effective managers, and even celebrated CEOs.

What separates the highly-focused individual from someone who's unable to concentrate for more than a few minutes? How do some people manage to master their attention when others seem to be at the mercy of every distraction?

By *training* themselves to do so.

Few people are born with the ability to focus. For most of us, it's a learned trait. A habit. That's great news because it means we can train ourselves to have singleminded focus when we need it. Like developing any good habit, it's just a matter of consistent application until it becomes so deeply-rooted that it's automatic.

Think about how true attention mastery will impact your life. You'll be able to finish tasks and projects on time. You'll be better able to do your best work. You'll make faster decisions with greater clarity and confidence. And you'll be truly *present* when you spend time with your family and friends.

And that's just the tip of the iceberg!

You've probably tried to improve your concentration at some

point in your life. Perhaps you've tried (and failed) multiple times. You're not alone. Most of us want to be more productive and effective. Mastering our attention is one of the surest paths toward effecting that goal.

The problem is, without a proven system to follow, such attempts usually end in failure and frustration. They certainly did for me. I'll bet you can relate from experience.

It's important to note that failure has great value. In fact, it's the best teacher in the world. We learn more from our failures than from any other outcome. They show us where to improve and give us the opportunity to do so.

Don't be afraid of failure. Embrace it! If you've attempted to improve your focus in the past and failed, try to figure out the reasons. Then, use that knowledge to move forward with purpose. (This action guide will show you how.)

Also, keep in mind that our ability to focus is limited. It's a resource we consume throughout the day, starting from the moment we wake up and lasting until the moment we go to bed. In that light, *managing* our focus is just as important as developing it in the first place. We'll talk more about focus management later in this book.

There are many ways to improve your concentration. But as you might suspect, some ways are better than others. *Fast Focus* explains the simplest, most effective plan I've come across. It's the one I use to this day. I use it because it works. I'm 100% confident it'll work for you, as well. If you put my plan into effect, you *will* learn to master your attention. I guarantee it.

I used to lack focus. It was difficult for me to concentrate on anything for more than a few minutes at a time. I was constantly surrendering to distractions, from email and news websites to social media and phone calls. Consequently, I had a difficult time getting things done.

My life changed when I began using the tactics and strategies described in this book. I learned to master my ability to concentrate, staying on task while ignoring distractions. I can now induce a state of focus whenever I need to.

The effects have literally been life-changing. I've written several books, maintain numerous websites, write a regular blog, and run a content marketing business while still having a life. When I'm with friends and loved ones, I'm present rather than distracted.

None of this would have been possible had I not implemented the system laid out in *Fast Focus*. The tactics that make up the system, many of them simple and some of them intuitive, have been instrumental in helping me to master my concentration. I'm certain you'll find them to be likewise invaluable - at work, at home, and in every activity you participate in.

In the next section, we'll talk about the ideas, hacks, and strategies that *Fast Focus* covers.

WHAT YOU'LL LEARN IN FAST FOCUS

∼

This action guide is broken down into three distinct parts. Each part examines an important facet of attention management.

The material we're going to cover in *Fast Focus* is organized in a way that'll make it easy for you to review later. Weeks from now, after you've read this book the entire way through, you'll want to revisit select pieces for a refresher. I've organized the three parts and their respective sections to simplify and hasten the process of finding the material you need *when you need it*. All you have to do is take a quick glance at the table of contents.

Here's a quick summary of what each of the three parts in *Fast Focus* covers:

Part I

Before we can discuss concepts like focus development and attention mastery, we need a framework through which to understand them. Part I will define what true focus means (the definition might surprise you) and explain why it's difficult to maintain.

We'll also take a look at common obstacles to attention management. When you know the challenges you'll face, they become less daunting and easier to overcome. Lastly, Part I will describe the many ways in which true focus - the ability to ignore internal and environmental distractions and stay on task - will enhance your life.

Part II

Your environment plays a crucial role in determining the extent to which you're able to concentrate. Part II will show you how to create an environment that not only minimizes distractions, but also puts you in a frame of mind where attention management is easier.

Part II will reveal the most important environmental factors you need to address, and show you how to adjust them to suit your needs.

Part III

In addition to creating an environment that helps you to concentrate, there are numerous tactics you can employ to sharpen your focus and stay on task. Part III of *Fast Focus* covers these tactics.

You'll learn 23 ways to fight distractions, master your attention, and get things done. Most of these tactics are universally effective; they work for everyone. It's just a matter of implementing them with consistency when you need to concentrate.

Bonus Material!

These days, more people than ever take their work to coffee shops like Starbucks. You've no doubt seen these folks. They're easy to spot with their laptops open and phones within easy reach. If you happen to be one of these road warriors, you know firsthand the challenges of ignoring distractions and staying on task.

In this bonus section, I'll give you several actionable tips to help you master your focus when you work in these venues. You'll learn how to ignore everything around you and boost your work productivity in the process.

As you can see, we're going to cover a lot of material in *Fast Focus*. But we're going to move through it quickly. If you've read any of my other books, you know that I place greater value on *actionable* advice than theory. To that end, the tips, tactics, and hacks you'll discover in *Fast Focus* are intended to be applied immediately.

If you apply them, I'm 100% confident you'll see measurable growth in your ability to focus and manage your attention. It doesn't matter if you're a student, a business owner, a senior executive, stay-at-home parent, or coach of your child's soccer team. The practices described throughout this book have been proven to work. They've worked for me. I'm confident they'll work for you, too.

Let's now talk about how you can get maximum value out of *Fast Focus*.

HOW TO SQUEEZE MAXIMUM VALUE FROM FAST FOCUS

~

As I mentioned, the advice you'll find throughout *Fast Focus* is meant to be applied. This book is filled to the brim with practical, *actionable* material designed for immediate use. I repeat this point for good reason. Inaction is one of the biggest challenges you'll face on the road toward developing razor-sharp focus.

Don't let *Fast Focus* sit on your Kindle, phone, or other reading device, gathering virtual dust. If you're holding the paperback version, don't just put it on your bookshelf and promise yourself that you'll read it when you have time.

Start reading it today. Begin your journey toward mastering your concentration.

Fast Focus is relatively short. That's by design. You don't need a 300-page book that plods along, weighed down by explorations into the psychology and neuroscience of attention management. As interesting as such topics are, they won't move the needle in terms of helping you to sharpen your focus.

Nor do you need a book filled with motivational, inspirational tripe. Motivation is fleeting. It's here today and gone tomorrow. It's helpful in the moment, but has a short shelf life. You need something enduring in its place that you can count on to encourage you to put the tips found in *Fast Focus* into practice.

In short, you need a fast-moving guide that provides a step-by-step, "how-to" blueprint for managing your attention. You need a *roadmap* that provides all of the tools required to develop and hone your focus, and then shows you exactly how to use them.

You're holding that roadmap now.

To get maximum value out of *Fast Focus*, commit to putting its tactics and hacks into action. Don't just read and forget them. These are the same practices I've used - and continue to use - to successfully fight distractions and zero in on my work. I'm using them right now as I write this. Experiment with them. Keep a journal detailing how they affect your ability to focus.

It's important to remember that you and I are different people. We work under different circumstances and almost certainly have different predilections. Some of the attention-mastery tactics that work for me may be less (or perhaps even more) effective for you. That's why it's important to experiment - to see which ones have the greatest impact on your ability to concentrate and keep distractions at bay.

Because here's the secret to getting the most out of *Fast Focus*: you must come up with a unique system that accommodates *your* needs, *your* strengths and weaknesses, and *your* desired lifestyle.

This book provides all of the tools you'll need to build that system. Along the way, I'll make suggestions on how to tailor your system to your circumstances.

Ready to roll up your sleeves and jump in? Let's do it!

PART I

LAYING THE GROUNDWORK

~

Before we can intelligently discuss focus development and attention management, we need to address a few fundamentals.

In Part I, we'll define focus and attention (prepare to be surprised) and talk about why both are difficult to master. We'll also discuss the most common obstacles to staying focused. Once you know what challenges to look for, you'll be better prepared to overcome them.

It's also important to know *why* you'd like to master your attention. The reasons may seem obvious to you. The problem is, that may dissuade you from truly examining them. If you neglect to investigate your "why," you risk never realizing the full range of benefits that accompany having a razor-sharp focus.

Part I resolves this problem from the outset. We'll take a look at the many positive effects attention mastery can have on your life.

FOCUS DEFINED!

~

People tend to think of focus as having tunnel vision. They believe it's the ability to ignore everything around them and zero in on the task sitting in front of them.

But focus and attention management are far more complicated than that. In reality, we manage different types of attention throughout each day. These different types dictate what we notice and don't notice, and what we ignore and choose not to ignore. They also have different uses and impose different challenges.

Confused? Rest assured, everything will become clear by the end of this section. Let's start by discussing voluntary versus involuntary attention.

Voluntary Vs. Involuntary Attention

These are the two main types of attention. Voluntary attention is what you use to consciously focus on something. For example, suppose you're reading a book in the same room in which your family is watching television. You may struggle to concentrate on the text. You have to consciously block out the noise around you in order to focus on your book.

That's voluntary attention. You control it. You decide what captures your notice and what doesn't.

Voluntary attention is like a muscle. Unfortunately, it's a muscle that has, for most of us, atrophied to the point of being useless. The good news is that voluntary attention can be strengthened through application. Like any muscle, it grows stronger with exercise. That means you can overcome distractions and develop the ability to concentrate on demand as long as you're willing to put in the work. *Fast Focus* takes you through this process.

Involuntary attention is the opposite of voluntary attention. You have no control over it. A gunshot will grab your attention regardless of how focused you are. Likewise, a blood-curdling scream will break your concentration, even if you're working in a flow state.

Involuntary attention has great value when our safety is at risk. Imagine our ancestors hunting for food. They would've been vulnerable to attacks from wild animals as well as from members of neighboring, aggressive tribes. Involuntary attention kept them alert, and thereby kept them safe (most of the time).

We're seldom in situations today that threaten our lives. We live in relative safety. We go about our days unconcerned that our lives might be put at risk at any given moment.

The problem is, our involuntary attention, an important part of our genetic makeup, is still there. It continues to work hard, drawing our attention to changes in our environment that might warrant our notice. But instead of wild animals and warring tribe members, it sounds the alarm over things that are trivial by comparison.

For example, your phone beeps, chirps, or vibrates, immediately drawing your attention and compelling you to check the reason. Or you notice that you've received a new email and immediately check to see who sent it. Or you notice a friend's Facebook updates and are unable to resist the temptation to read them.

That's your involuntary attention at work. It has less use today since our lives aren't under constant threat (most of us, anyway). But it continues to toil in the background, trying to earn its keep. Unfortunately, it only succeeds in creating an endless stream of distractions.

The takeaway is that voluntary attention and involuntary attention are different mechanisms. You control the former, but have little to no control over the latter. Note that you dampen the influence of involuntary attention by exercising more control over voluntary attention. We'll talk more about this throughout *Fast Focus*.

Let's now define the difference between broad and focused attention.

Broad Vs. Focused Attention

Broad attention allows you to evaluate circumstances from a bird's-eye view. You use it to see the forest rather than the trees.

For example, suppose you're a general in a theater of war working on military strategy. You'd use broad attention to map out strike plans, envision supply lines, and forecast the movements of large groups of troops, including those of your adversaries.

Or suppose you're the coach of your son or daughter's basketball team and you're creating a game strategy. You'd use broad attention to predict the myriad of situations your players might find themselves in, and devise appropriate responses.

The best way to think of broad attention is that it provides the big picture. Once you have a grasp of your overall situation, you can apply *focused* attention to address the details.

Focused attention allows you to appraise specific situations and come up with the most suitable approaches given your resources and goals.

Let's again suppose you're a general working on military strategy. A challenge you might face is how to overtake a particular area in a war theater given the strength and number of your adversary. You'd use focused attention to resolve this challenge.

Or let's again suppose you're the coach of your child's basketball team. It's near the end of the fourth quarter with 10 seconds on the clock, and your players are up by two points. The problem is, the opposing team has a player who excels in sinking three-pointers. You'd use focused attention to create an effective three-point defense strategy.

The good news about broad attention and focused attention is that both are in your control. Unlike involuntary attention, you decide how to best wield them to your advantage.

Keep in mind, both broad attention and focused attention pose potential pitfalls. For example, concentrating only on the big picture (broad attention) will allow important details to fall through the cracks. Zeroing in on specific situations (focused attention) to the exclusion of the big picture can lead to tunnel vision, impairing your overall awareness.

I ADMIT, this has been a relatively long section. But having a full appreciation of the different types of attention, as well as how they work, will prove useful as you learn to develop and sharpen your focus.

In the following section, we'll take a quick look at the most common reasons we tend to lose focus.

WHY WE LOSE FOCUS

~

You know the feeling.

You have a lot of work to get done, but you're unable to concentrate on it. You're distracted. Every noise you hear, from your phone notifications to the sound of traffic outside, pulls your attention away from the task at hand. And when you finally complete your work, you have the nagging feeling that its quality has suffered due to your lack of focus.

Sound familiar? That's the experience I went through, again and again, before I learned to master my attention. It's deeply frustrating. I know firsthand.

In order to strengthen our focus, it's important to appreciate why we lose it in the first place. It usually comes down to these five factors:

1. Lack of interest
2. Negative emotions
3. Poor organization
4. Low energy levels

5. Lack of control

Let's take a quick look at each one.

Lack Of Interest

It's easier to concentrate when you're interested in the item you're trying to concentrate on. Focus requires feeling engaged by the task in front of you. You need to feel stimulated. When you're interested in your work, you're more likely to zero in on it and ignore the distractions around you.

Negative Emotions

A negative emotional state will erode your ability to concentrate. If you're feeling stressed, annoyed, lonely, depressed, or hostile, you'll find it impossible to focus. That's human nature. Your mind will be so preoccupied with these emotions that it'll leave few cognitive resources available for managing your attention.

Poor Organization

Show me someone who follows a structured day and I'll show you someone who's able to concentrate and successfully ignore distractions.

It's easier to manage your attention when your day follows a consistent, familiar pattern. With good organization, you'll be better able to keep chaos at bay. That in turn will help you to stay focused on whatever you're working on.

Low Energy Levels

Low energy is the attention-dampening factor that people most often overlook. Prolonged focus requires a lot of energy, which comes by way of good food, sufficient sleep, and regular exercise. The problem is, many of us neglect one or more of these elements. We eat unhealthy food, sacrifice sleep for other priorities, and spend too little time moving our bodies.

Your brain is the linchpin in developing attention mastery and maintaining focus. It can't function properly without sufficient energy.

Lack Of Control

How you control your time determines how well you're able to concentrate. If you allow people to interrupt you at their whim, you'll never achieve the flow state necessary to work unencumbered by distractions. You'll never feel fully immersed in the task at hand.

You must control your time if you hope to develop razor-sharp focus. Admittedly, it's not always feasible. Some interruptions are impossible to avoid. But most of us can take steps to improve in this area.

Is Mind Wandering Always Bad?

When you lose focus, your mind wanders. But is this always a bad thing?

Absolutely not. The key is to make it work for you.

Mind wandering allows your brain to be creative. To that end, it can help you to identify nontraditional solutions to problems that have proven difficult to resolve.

This doesn't mean you should allow your mind to wander at every opportunity. That's sure to impose a cost on your performance and productivity.

Focus when your circumstances require you to do so. That's what this book will train you to do. But when you're taking a shower, exercising at the gym, or taking a walk, allow your brain the freedom to wander. You may be surprised by where it leads you.

You're now familiar with the five biggest factors that cause us to lose focus during any given day. In the next section, we'll drill down to the 10 most common obstacles we face in *staying* focused.

TOP 10 OBSTACLES TO STAYING FOCUSED

~

There are two aspects to managing your attention: honing in on whatever you're working on and staying focused during the time you've allotted to it.

In order to stay focused, you have to be aware of the condition your mind is in. For example, it's difficult to concentrate if you're tired, stressed, or agitated.

The truth is, there are *numerous* factors that can impair your ability to stay focused. This section will cover the 10 that pose the biggest challenges.

Obstacle #1 - Mental Fatigue

If your brain is exhausted, you'll find it's almost impossible to focus. You'll be prone to distractions, one after another, which will prevent you from zeroing in on the task in front of you.

Mental exhaustion can stem from several factors, but the most common one is failing to get sufficient sleep. Even if you manage to get to bed at a decent time, you might toss and turn all night. That'll rob your brain of the restful slumber it needs to prepare itself for the following day.

Obstacle #2 - Restlessness

Restlessness is defined as a general feeling of anxiety. Something is causing you to feel ill at ease. Your brain receives signals that everything is not as it should be, and devotes cognitive resources to investigating and resolving the issue.

The problem is, it's often difficult to identify the reasons we feel restless. Consequently, the brain spins its wheels trying to resolve something it's unable to pinpoint. As you can imagine, this has a negative impact on your ability to manage your attention.

Obstacle #3 - Stress

A little stress is good for us. It keeps us alert. It can even help us to hone our focus. But many people (perhaps you?) suffer from *chronic* stress. They're in a constant state of anxiety.

This persistent stress can stem from many causes. Some people feel stressed when they lack control over their day. Others become stressed when deadlines approach and they feel unprepared to meet them. Still others undergo significant life events, such as a divorce or the passing of a loved one, that cause them stress.

Stress erodes your attention. The more you feel and the longer you feel it, the less you'll be able to concentrate.

Obstacle #4 - Interruptions

Have you ever tried to concentrate on something only to be hampered by a continuous string of interruptions (coworkers, phone calls, etc.)? It's frustrating. Not only does each interruption destroy your momentum, but it takes 20 minutes to get back on track.

That's the reason it's so difficult to focus when people interrupt you over and over.

Obstacle #5 - Lack Of Mental Clarity

Our brains are oftentimes filled with trivial thoughts and ideas that have nothing to do with the work in front of us. These thoughts and ideas constitute mental clutter.

The clutter makes it difficult to concentrate. A cluttered mind is an unfocused mind.

Obstacle #6 - Unresolved Problems

An unresolved problem is like a leaky faucet that prevents you from falling asleep at night. It's there, in the background, calling attention to itself. It refuses to go away, which causes your brain to devote attentional resources to it.

For example, suppose you and your spouse had an explosive argument last night that remains unsettled. Or suppose the investments in your retirement fund needs to be adjusted in light of how certain sectors are underperforming.

It's difficult to concentrate when such unresolved problems hang over our heads and nag us.

Obstacle #7 - Poor Planning

It's tough to focus on a task or project when you lack a clear, methodical plan to follow. Your brain will jump into action and attempt to fill in the gaps. The problem is, it's unskilled at doing so.

For example, recall the last time you visited a grocery store without a grocery list. Your attention was no doubt drawn to numerous items as you walked down each aisle, some out of curiosity and others out of need. The visit, which would have taken 10 minutes had you arrived with a list, probably took much longer.

That's your brain working without a plan. It's in an unfocused state.

Obstacle #8 - Physical Clutter

Take a look at your workspace. Is it tidy or messy? Is it an example of control or chaos?

Physical clutter in your work environment will impair your focus. While many people claim they're able to concentrate while working in a messy environment, studies say different. In 2011, the *Journal of Neuroscience* published a report examining the effect of clutter on attention management.[1] The authors noted the following:

> "Multiple stimuli present in the visual field at the same time compete for neural representation by mutually suppressing their evoked activity throughout visual cortex, providing a neural correlate for the limited processing capacity of the visual system."

That's a fancy way of saying that a messy desk hampers your ability to concentrate.

Obstacle #9 - Social Media

Recent research purports that social media has no long-term effect on our ability to concentrate.[2] But according to numerous *past* studies, it most certainly has a negative *short-term* effect. One study, published in the journal *Computers In Human Behavior*, demonstrated that students couldn't go more than *few minutes* without checking Facebook, Instagram, Twitter, and other social sites.[3]

No wonder so many students pull all-nighters to get things done!

Social media sites pose a significant distraction. If you're unable to resist them, you'll find it very difficult to focus on your work.

Obstacle #10 - Your Phone

It shouldn't be a surprise that our phones hobble our focus, even when we're not looking at them. They constantly ring, chirp, and vibrate, notifying us of incoming texts, voicemails, and social media updates.

In the context of attention management, trying to focus with your phone within earshot is a recipe for failure. You know this from experience. When you hear your phone chirp or feel it vibrate, it's difficult to resist reaching for it to identify the reason. Even if you manage to ignore the notifications, they'll disrupt your momentum and cause your mind to wander.

NOTICE that I haven't offered any tactical solutions to the 10 obstacles highlighted above. There's a good reason. If you follow the advice presented in *Fast Focus*, you'll overcome these challenges as a natural result.

What If You've Been Diagnosed With ADHD?

If you've been diagnosed with Attention Deficit Hyperactivity Disorder (ADHD), I urge you to seek the guidance of a medical professional. This action guide is designed to provide neither medical nor psychiatric advice. Your doctor is far better suited to recommend compensatory strategies for sharpening your focus if you have ADHD. Such strategies may include meditation, behavioral therapy, and even prescription medications.

NOW THAT YOU'RE aware of the biggest obstacles to staying focused, let's take a look at how mastering your attention will positively affect your life.

------

1. https://www.ncbi.nlm.nih.gov/pubmed/21228167
2. http://www.inderscienceonline.com/doi/abs/10.1504/IJSMILE.2016.079505
3. http://www.sciencedirect.com/science/article/pii/S0747563212003305

7 WAYS IMPROVED FOCUS WILL POSITIVELY AFFECT YOUR LIFE

~

The ability to focus impacts our lives in a myriad of ways. Writers, artists, and musicians stand to produce a greater volume of work with increased passion and personal investment. Teachers and professors can more easily create lectures, assignments, and exams that are tailored to help their students excel. Parents will find it easier to come up with fun, creative, and educational activities for their children.

In short, it's our chronic *lack* of focus - the inability to concentrate - that produces uninspiring results in everything we do.

It doesn't have to be that way. You can learn to manage your attention. In fact, by the time you finish reading this action guide, you'll have the tools you need to concentrate whenever you need to.

With that in mind, let's explore seven ways in which mastering your focus will improve your quality of life. As you read through each of them, consider how each might impact the quality of your work, the volume of your output, and the connections you share with others.

Let's start with your ability to get important things done on time.

#1 - Increased Productivity

Focus allows you to ignore distractions and stay on task. You're thus better able to achieve a flow state, where your attention is completely absorbed by the task in front of you.

Working in a flow state leads to higher productivity. You're able to direct your attention and block distracting stimuli that would otherwise break your concentration and cripple your momentum. Accordingly, you'll get more done in less time.

#2 - Improved Relationships

When we neglect to manage our attention, we invariably spread ourselves too thin. Consequently, we leave ourselves with too little time, energy, and attentional resources to offer the people we love and value.

When you learn to control your attention, you'll find that you're more present when you spend time with friends and loved ones. You'll enjoy stronger connections with them, more trust and intimacy, and as a result experience a greater sense of fulfillment.

#3 - Boost In Critical Thinking

Critical thinking isn't just something you do in college. It can benefit you throughout your life.

For example, when you read a novel, you'll feel more immersed in the story. When you read non-fiction, you'll be better able to absorb and apply unfamiliar concepts. If you're in a position to render judgement - for example, to settle a squabble between your kids - you'll be able to do so with fairness and reason.

Focus is required to think critically. Master the former and you'll improve the latter.

#4 - More Grit

Experts claim that intelligence is a poor barometer of success. Instead, one of the best gauges of whether a person will overcome life's inevitable challenges is his or her resilience, or grit. With it, there's a greater likelihood of success in everything he or she does.

Grit demands sharp focus. It requires zeroing in on the challenge in question and devoting more cognitive and physical resources to overcoming it. Learn to direct your attention and you'll become more resilient to the challenges you'll undoubtedly confront during any given day.

#5 - Greater Decisiveness

Decisiveness is the ability to make decisions without overanalyzing things. It doesn't mean being impulsive. Rather, it allows you to evaluate your circumstances, consider your varied options, and choose one with confidence.

Decisiveness is a crucial skill, whether you're a teacher, military leader, corporate executive, or stay-at-home parent. Importantly, it's a skill that can be developed. The one essential ingredient is attention mastery. The ability to make good decisions with confidence and without hesitance requires being able to focus on the problem at hand.

#6 - Better Retention Of New Information

Have you ever had difficulty remembering new details, such as a person's name, an unfamiliar concept, or the best route to a particular destination? Of course. All of us have.

Many factors affect our ability to retain information. They include our stress levels, the amount of sleep we enjoy each night, and our energy levels. Energy levels are further influenced by diet, exercise, physical ailments, and other factors.

Having said that, the greatest impact on your retention of new information comes via your ability to focus. It's what allows you to ignore distractions, cut through brain fog, and concentrate on whatever details you're trying to commit to memory.

#7 - Improved Self-Confidence

Take another look at the six benefits we've just covered. Imagine mastering your attention to the point that you experience all six. How would that affect your self-confidence?

You'll feel as if you can accomplish anything you set your mind to. Imagine enjoying increased productivity, stronger relationships, an ability to think critically, more resilience, better decision-making, and an improved memory. You'll feel more self-assured whenever you undertake a new task or project!

YOU NOW KNOW what's at stake. You recognize the many ways in which the ability to focus when needed can lead to a more rewarding lifestyle.

It's time for a pop quiz. In the next section, let's find out if you truly have a focus problem, and if you do, its severity.

POP QUIZ: DO YOU TRULY HAVE A FOCUS PROBLEM?

~

I
t's safe to say that most of us struggle with focus. There's so much engaging stimuli around us, from our phone apps to the internet, that managing our attention for long periods is a constant challenge.

Having said that, some of us suffer more than others. We're more vulnerable to distractions. We're more inclined to set aside important work to answer the siren call of texts, email, and social media.

It's important to realize that every distraction sidetracks us, no matter how harmless it seems. Each one breaks our concentration and disrupts our momentum. To that end, they wreak havoc with our productivity and greatly impact the quality of our work.

So let's discover the extent to which you have difficulty concentrating. Below, you'll find 15 statements. Score yourself from one (1) to five (5) according to how true these statements are in your life. A score of one indicates that a statement perfectly describes you. A score of five indicates that it's entirely untrue.

At the end, we'll tally the results to determine how big of a problem focus is for you.

1. You become restless or fidgety while working on tasks.
2. You work on multiple tasks or projects at the same time.
3. You regularly fail to notice important details.
4. You neglect to plan your day.
5. You quickly become bored.
6. You're easily distracted.
7. Your mind wanders during meetings.
8. You neglect to set daily goals and objectives.
9. You're absentminded and tend to forget things.
10. Your workspace is filled with clutter.
11. Irrelevant thoughts constantly surface while you're working.
12. You find it difficult to focus on what people are saying during conversations.
13. Your mornings, afternoons, and evenings don't follow defined routines.
14. You often forget where you place personal items.
15. You routinely arrive late to meetings and appointments.

AGAIN, give yourself a score between one and five for each of the 15 statements. Then, add up your points.

If your cumulative score is **between 60 and 75**, you enjoy better control over your attention than most people. You're able to easily ignore distractions. You're also capable of reaching a flow state when you work (assuming you're interested in the task or project in front of you). Frankly, you may not need to finish reading *Fast Focus*. I recommend doing so, however, as you're likely to learn at least a few tips that'll help bump your score even higher!

If you scored **between 45 and 59 points**, you're reasonably successful at managing your attention, but doing so consistently remains a challenge. Reading this action guide will definitely help you to improve your focus. Along the way, you'll almost certainly reap the benefits described in the previous section.

If your score is **between 30 and 44**, it signals that staying focused is a persistent challenge for you. You have difficulty concentrating on your work, your studies, and activities. You lose track of what people are saying when they're speaking to you. You're unable to concentrate for long periods because you're ultra-susceptible to distractions in your immediate environment. The tips you'll learn throughout *Fast Focus* will bring about marked improvement in these and many other areas of your life.

If you scored **less than 30**, there's considerable work to be done. Mastering your attention will require consistent application of solid advice. The good news is that you're holding the only guide you'll ever need. By the time you finish reading it, you'll have the necessary tools to trigger razor-sharp focus on demand. Whether you're a student, professor, corporate manager, entrepreneur, or stay-at-home parent, attention mastery will help you to design the lifestyle you crave.

It's now time to address one of the most commonly-overlooked aspects with regard to fighting distractions and developing laser-like concentration: your work environment.

PART II

HOW TO CREATE AN ENVIRONMENT THAT HELPS YOU TO FOCUS

∽

Your environment plays a huge role in determining whether you're able to concentrate for extended periods. A supportive environment can help you to more easily avoid distractions, focus on your work, and even enter a flow state. The *wrong* environment can make it nearly impossible to manage your attention for more than a few fleeting moments.

In the following sections, we'll explore the environmental factors that have the greatest impact on your ability to focus. If you address these 11 factors properly, you'll be astonished at how easily you can zero in on your work and how efficiently you can get things done.

LIGHTING

~

You need proper lighting to manage your attention. Studies consistently show that young people are better able to concentrate when they work in a well-lit environment.[1] [2]

This same effect can be observed in adults who work in offices. Low-light conditions negatively affect their mood, focus, and productivity. When they have plenty of light, they're happier and more mentally engaged, both of which make concentration easier.

You know this from experience.

Recall the last time you tried to read and absorb new material when you had insufficient light. Did you have difficulty remembering passages or comprehending new concepts? Did you find your attention wavering or start feeling drowsy? Did you experience eye strain that distracted you from the material?

That's to be expected when you work in a poorly-lit workspace.

When I was in college, I would study in the campus library. It had terrible lighting. I'd arrive with the best of intentions, find an available table, and 30 minutes later, without fail, find myself staring into space. Sometimes, I'd fall asleep.

Because of this issue, learning new material and studying for exams took longer than necessary. I logged a lot of hours in that library, but much of that time was wasted.

This was years before I learned how to master my attention. It was also long before I understood the effect of lighting on my ability to concentrate.

When you sit down to work, note the amount of light available in your surroundings. If it's insufficient, find another location.

Also, take advantage of natural light whenever possible. Studies show that natural light improves both workplace performance and productivity.[3] [4]

---

1. Nienke M. Moolenaar, Mirjam Galetzka, and Ad Pruyn, Lighting affects students' concentration positively: Findings from three Dutch studies, *Lighting Research and Technology* (2013)
2. http://sgo.sagepub.com/content/2/2/2158244012445585
3. https://www.ncbi.nlm.nih.gov/pmc/articles/PMC4031400/
4. http://www.nrel.gov/docs/fy02osti/30769.pdf (page 10, Productivity in the Office)

BACKGROUND NOISE

~

I f you're easily distracted, any type of noise near your workspace can weaken your concentration. Voices nearby can sidetrack you from your work. Repetitive clicking, tapping, and ringing can draw your attention, much like a leaky faucet might prevent you from falling asleep.

Background noise can make it impossible to stay on task. The question to ask yourself is whether *all* types of noise break your concentration, or just certain types.

For example, you might be easily distracted by the sound of conversation, but able to focus while listening to classical music. Your attention may be easily diverted by the intermittent sounds produced by video games, but not the continuous thrum of a building's air conditioner.

Some people need absolute silence in order to focus. Others do better with ambient noise, such as white noise, brown noise, or pink noise. Still others find they can best zero in on their work when there's a constant buzz of activity around them. And some folks feel most relaxed and productive while working with the sounds of wind and rain in the background. (I've included links below to online resources you can use to recreate these sounds.)

Everyone's different. Experiment with different types of background noise to see which ones work best for *you*.

First, spend 30 minutes working in total silence. Take notes on how doing so affects your attention.

Next, work for 30 minutes while listening to baroque music (Bach and Vivaldi are great options). Again, take notes regarding its influence on you.

Next, try working with white noise, brown noise, and pink noise in the background. How does each one affect your ability to concentrate?

The key to making this work is to take notes so you can compare the results. You'll eventually find the type of background noise that best suits you.

Also, keep in mind that different types of noise may be ideally suited to specific types of work. If you're creating something - for example, writing an essay or painting a portrait - you might find instrumental jazz music to be an ideal accompaniment. However, if you're trying to learn new material, you may find silence works best.

The only way to find out what works for you is to experiment. Remember, *you* control the background noise in your environment. If it isn't to your liking, use the resources below to create the backdrop of sound that best helps you to manage your attention.

If you need silence, consider investing in a durable pair of noise-canceling headphones or earbuds. (Ear plugs are less than ideal because most block only 33 dB of sound. That's not nearly enough to mimic silence.)

Resources:

Ambient noise
  https://simplynoise.com/

Constant buzz of activity
  https://coffitivity.com/

Wind and rain sounds
  http://www.rainymood.com/
  http://asoftmurmur.com/

COMFORT

~

I t shouldn't be a surprise that your comfort affects your ability to concentrate. If you're uncomfortable, whether due to your chair, the position of your desk, or a physical ailment, remaining focused for long periods will be all but impossible.

Think about the many aspects that contribute to - or detract from - your comfort while you work. Following are several examples:

- The height of your chair and desk
- The fit of your shoes
- The fit of your clothes
- Your sitting posture
- How much time you spend sitting without a break
- The position of your monitor in relation to your line of sight

These factors dictate whether you feel comfortable at your

workstation (or on your couch if you work at home). They thus play a significant role in determining whether you're able to focus.

Consider each one in light of your work environment. Is your chair comfy? Is it set at the correct height given the height of your workstation? (Your arms should form 90-degree angles at the elbows.) Are your shoes too tight? Do your clothes fit properly?

Next, examine your posture...

- Is your back straight with your shoulders back?
- Is your backside touching the back of your chair?
- Are your feet planted flat on the ground?
- Are your knees bent at a 90-degree angle?
- Is your weight distributed evenly across both hips?
- Is the normal curvature of your back evident as you sit?

Consider the contours and makeup of your chair...

- Is the padding so plush that it causes you to feel drowsy?
- Does it constantly roll, forcing you use your feet and core muscles to maintain your position in front of your monitor?
- Does it provide sufficient support for your back and hips?
- Does it offer enough breathability?
- Does it support proper sitting posture? (See above)
- Does it allow you to adjust the arm rests, back support, and other features according to your body's needs?

Measure the distance between your monitor and your eyes. The ideal distance is between 24 and 36 inches. The top of your monitor should be at the same height as your sight line.

If your monitor is above or below your sight line, even by a few inches, you'll experience neck strain and eyestrain. Both will severely hamper your comfort. That in turn will compromise your focus.

Keep in mind, sitting for extended periods can cause discomfort, even if you own an ergonomic chair, maintain proper sitting posture, and enjoy an optimized workspace. Stand and stretch every 30 minutes. Take a short walk. Doing so will relieve the tension in your neck and shoulders, allowing you to return to your work feeling refreshed and ready to focus.

AMBIENT TEMPERATURE

~

I can't focus when my workspace is too warm. I could be on trial for a crime I didn't commit, and if the courtroom is too warm, I'm almost certain to doze off.

One of my college professors preferred to keep his room warm. One day, after watching me nod off to sleep - a daily occurrence made worse by the fact that I sat in the front row - he confronted me. "Damon, you fall asleep in class every single day. Is everything okay at home?" he asked.

I didn't have the mindfulness to tell him to turn the heater down. So, this sad routine continued for the remainder of the semester.

I'm not alone in this. And neither are you if you react similarly in a too-warm environment.

The employment goliath CareerBuilder sponsored a survey in 2015 wherein it asked thousands of full-time workers to describe the temperature in their offices and its effect on their productivity.[1] Twenty-five percent claimed their offices were too warm. Twenty-three percent claimed they were too cold.

Seventy-one percent of workers surveyed claimed that working in a too-warm office had a negative impact on their productivity. Fifty-three percent said working in an office that was too *cold* had a similar effect.

These findings were similar to those from a month-long study conducted by Cornell over a decade ago.[2] The researchers found the sweet spot in terms of ambient temperature to be between 68 and 77 degrees Fahrenheit. Workers performed with the highest degree of productivity and made the least number of errors in that temperature range. When the temperature dropped below 68 degrees or rose above 77 degrees, their productivity plummeted and their error rate climbed.

Clearly, the temperature in your workspace can have a major effect on your ability to concentrate and work productively. The key is knowing how to manage it. You won't always be able to control the thermostat in your environment. Here are a few compensatory ideas in the event you need to improvise:

- Dress in layers. If it's too warm, you can remove them until you feel comfortable.
- Bring a small floor fan or desk fan to your office to stay cool. Bring a small space heater to stay warm.
- Have liquid cold gel packs readily available. Place them under the soles of your feet when you feel too warm.
- Sip iced water to keep your internal temperature under control.
- If you need a desk lamp, use one with an LED bulb rather than a heat-generating incandescent bulb.
- Open a window if the air outside is cooler than the air within your office.
- Bring a light blanket or sweater to the office if the thermostat is routinely set too low.

- Carry a lightweight scarf you can drape around your neck.

The goal is to effect an ambient temperature that keeps you alert and focused. Use the ideas above to warm yourself or cool yourself as circumstances warrant.

---

1. http://www.prnewswire.com/news-releases/temperature-wars-are-heating-up-the-workplace-according-to-new-careerbuilder-survey-300194019.html
2. http://ergo.human.cornell.edu/Conferences/EECE_IEQ%20and%20Productivity_ABBR.pdf

AIR QUALITY

~

Would you believe the air inside a venue can be more polluted than the air outside? Worse, this sad reality is common according to the Environmental Protection Agency (EPA). Copiers, printers, office furniture, and various chemicals found in different types of flooring and paint release pollutants. Research also shows that prolonged exposure to high levels of carbon dioxide has a negative impact on workers' performance.[1]

We rarely, if ever, notice such pollutants because they're invisible to the naked eye. But for many people, they cause a variety of physical reactions, such as headaches, fatigue, and even nausea. Some also trigger allergies.

These and other reactions will negatively affect your ability to focus. As such, they hurt your productivity. According to the Occupational Safety and Health Administration (OSHA), employers lose $15 billion a year to worker inefficiency and sick leave attributable to poor air quality.

The question is, what can you do about it?

If you work in an office, you have little control over the ventilation system and air quality in your environment. Your best option is to take frequent breaks outside. Take a short walk. Get some sun. Breathe fresh air. A side benefit of taking frequent breaks is that it'll prevent you from sitting too long.

If you're a student, you might have more flexibility based on your class schedule. Take advantage of breaks between classes to go outside. Don't spend your free time cooped up in the library where you're likely to breathe bad air. Find an isolated spot outside if you need to study. Wear headphones if you need to drown out environmental noise.

If you're an entrepreneur, novelist, freelancer, or stay-at-home parent, you have more freedom. You can change your environment whenever you want (exceptions aside). Take advantage of that latitude. Take frequent breaks and venture outdoors to enjoy the fresh air.

While your options may be limited, you *do* have them. Take advantage of them. The upside is that you'll be more focused and better able to fight distractions even as the poor air quality in your workspace tries to erode your attention.

---

1. https://www.hsph.harvard.edu/news/press-releases/green-office-environments-linked-with-higher-cognitive-function-scores/

SCENTS

~

Some smells distract us while others help us to concentrate. For example, recall the last time you tried to work with the pungent smell of fish wafting under your nose. You probably found it difficult to focus. The aroma may not be unpleasant to you. It's just so strong that it's a distraction.

Now, recall the last time you worked with a hint of peppermint or cinnamon in the air. These scents are known to *aid* concentration.

The aromas and odors to which we're exposed affect our mood and disposition. Consequently, they affect our ability to manage our attention and stay on task.

Most people realize this, both intuitively and from experience. But did you know there are several scents that can improve your mood, help you to focus, and boost your productivity?

Here are a few examples (I already mentioned the first two scents):

- Peppermint

- Cinnamon
- Pine
- Rosemary
- Basil
- Citrus
- Lavender
- Cypress

These savors are known to help increase alertness and prevent fatigue. For example, rosemary can help clear your head, making you less vulnerable to distractions. Peppermint stimulates the brain and improves concentration. Citrus and cinnamon help reduce mental fatigue. Both also uplift your mood.

How do produce these scents? With candles, oils, and even incense.

Of course, your work environment will dictate the amount of latitude you have with using these items. For example, if you work in an office with other people, you may not have the freedom to light candles, heat scented oils, or burn incense. Your coworkers might complain. Or worse, they'll stay silent, but hold a grudge.

An alternative is to keep a towel or wash cloth handy. When you need a mood lift, place a few drops of scented oil on the cloth, place the cloth over your nose, and inhale.

It's an imperfect solution, but still effective.

Of course, if you work at home, you can use the above methods - candles, oils, and incense - at your leisure. Experiment with the aromas I've listed above. Note which ones have the greatest effect on your mood, alertness, and ability to concentrate.

If you spend a lot of time in public venues, such as libraries or coffeeshops, you obviously won't be able to light candles or burn incense (at least, not without drawing glares). In the event you're bombarded with odors that distract you, your best option is to move.

For example, suppose the man sitting near you neglected to put on deodorant after visiting the gym. Or suppose the lady at the neighboring table is wearing enough perfume to knock out an elephant. In these cases, try to relocate to another table. If doing so isn't an option, it's best to leave the venue and work elsewhere. You're unlikely to get any substantive work done while being assailed by such "fragrances."

PRESENCE OF OTHERS

~

Conversation, laughter, and the sounds of kids playing are concentration busters. As I mentioned earlier, we're social creatures, and naturally drawn to others. When we hear people talking, we're curious about the topics. When we hear laughter, we want to find out the reason. When we hear children playing, we're drawn toward their youthful exuberance.

I'm not ashamed to say that I've eavesdropped on more than my share of conversations. And whenever I hear laughter, a part of me will always wonder what I'm missing.

That's human nature. Unfortunately, this penchant makes attention mastery difficult, if not impossible. I'm certain you can relate. Recall the last time you tried to stay on task while overhearing coworkers discussing a new film you wanted to see. Your attention was probably drawn to the conversation, relegating the task in front of you to a lower (immediate) priority.

What are your options when you're trying to concentrate, but are distracted by others in your vicinity? Here are a few ideas:

- Move to another location.
- Put on noise-canceling headphones.
- Play instrumental music or white noise through your headphones.
- Take a break outside and hope the offending parties will have left by the time you've returned.

You can also ask the offending parties to lower their voices or relocate. That's a less-than-ideal option for two reasons. First, the offending parties may become angry and respond accordingly. Second, it forces you to rely on the goodwill of others, who may prove to be stubborn.

If you work from home or you're a stay-at-home parent, you'll be better able to control the the level of noise generated by others. For example, you can ask your children to play board games rather than loud video games. If your spouse is home, you can ask him or her to avoid disturbing you for a set period of time.

You have fewer options if you work in an office environment because you have less influence over others. After all, they're not your family. They're probably going to be more cavalier regarding your need for silence. In that case, relocating, wearing noise-canceling headphones, listening to relaxing instrumental music, and taking a break are your best bets.

ORGANIZATION

~

The manner in which you organize your workspace will influence your ability to focus. The position of your desk, filing cabinets, and other office furniture in relation to your office door and windows will either help you to stay on task or distract you.

For example, suppose your office is cramped. The limited space can make you feel claustrophobic, a feeling that'll whittle away at your concentration.

Or suppose your desk faces a window that looks out upon a sidewalk where people regularly walk by. The constant movement will distract you.

Or suppose your chair is positioned so that your back faces your office door. If you leave your door open, you may be nagged by the ever-present possibility that someone is looking over your shoulder. This too can break your concentration.

How can you organize your office or workspace in a way that allows you to focus on your work? Following are a few ideas.

- Get rid of furniture you don't need. If you have a couch in your office that's rarely used, remove it. The extra space will give you mental breathing room.
- Organize your office to streamline traffic flow. For example, there should be no obstacles positioned between your desk and the door.
- Dedicate one desk tray for all incoming items. No more than one.
- Make certain you have sufficient light. Whether you're using overhead lights or a desk lamp, good lighting is essential to maintaining your focus.
- Organize your desk drawers so you know exactly where to find paper clips, rubber bands, stamps, and other items.
- Remove books and magazines from your desktop. Discard them, give them away, or keep them on a bookshelf.
- Use a single container (a cup will suffice) to hold pens, pencils, scissors, and similar items you need throughout the day.
- Invest in a larger trash can. The larger the trash can, the less often you'll need to break your momentum to empty it. Don't be afraid to sacrifice aesthetics for utility.
- Remove recreational items from your workspace. Designate the space for work only. Keep your phone, iPad, Kindle, and other gadgets elsewhere. Designate a zone for work. Designate a separate zone for play.
- If you use a filing cabinet to store documents, consider storing everything in the cloud using services like Evernote, Dropbox, Microsoft OneDrive, Google Drive, or Box. The goal is to eventually get rid of the filing cabinet, opening up the physical space it occupies.

The better organized I am, the better I'm able to concentrate. I strongly recommend organizing your workspace in a way that allows you to mentally breathe. You'll find that doing so will help you to better manage your attention and keep distractions at bay.

CLUTTER

~

I magine that you're sitting at your desk, ready to get to work. You're motivated and armed with a carefully-planned to-do list. You feel today is going to be ultra-productive.

Then, you notice the miscellany strewn across your desk's surface. Pens, documents, a stapler, rulers, and countless paper clips and rubber bands litter the area. Folders that should have been filed or discarded days ago sit in a disorderly pile (or worse, multiple piles). Books and magazines that haven't been opened in weeks add to the disarray. Somewhere under the mess lies your keyboard. But that's more of a hope than a certainty.

You can feel your motivation slowly drain away. The clutter distracts you. It makes it difficult to concentrate. You hear a nagging voice in your head telling you that the chaos on your desk is unacceptable.

You're not alone. Millions of people try to get work done on messy desks. Unfortunately, according to scientists, they're severely hampering their ability to focus.

In the section *Top 10 Obstacles To Staying Focused*, I mentioned a study published in the *Journal of Neuroscience* in 2011. I'll repeat the authors' findings for easy reference:

 "Multiple stimuli present in the visual field at the same time compete for neural representation by mutually suppressing their evoked activity throughout visual cortex, providing a neural correlate for the limited processing capacity of the visual system."

Clutter pulls at your attention. It distracts you, even if you don't realize it's happening. Worse, it diminishes your brain's ability to process information. Your memory suffers. Your comprehension suffers. The speed with which you absorb new material declines.

You can imagine how this might affect your concentration, and ultimately impact your work quality and productivity.

Because clutter can wreck your ability to focus, it's worth taking steps to remove as much clutter as possible from your workspace. Here are a few ideas to get you started:

- Make a list of every item you'll need to complete your work in the time allotted. Keep these items within reach.
- Remove all other items from your desk. Place them into a single box, and set the box aside. This allows you to regain focus immediately. Organize or discard the items in the box after you've completed your work.
- Organize the drawers of your desk according to the importance of the items they contain. Place items you use every day, such as paper clips and rubber bands, in the top drawer. Place rulers, scissors, and colored markers - items you might regularly use, but not every day - in the middle drawer. File old invoices

that you refer to only occasionally in the bottom
drawer.

- Arrange the cables on your desk so they're out of sight.
  You can purchase a number of tools, such as rain
  gutters, clamps, and cable management kits, for this
  purpose.
- Place your computer tower and printer under your
  desk rather than on top of it.

The above suggestions are merely the tip of the iceberg. The
main point is that you remove as much clutter as possible from
your workspace.

You'll feel more relaxed. You'll feel more creative. And your
brain will be better able to zero in on your work rather than
being constantly distracted by disarray.

TIME INDICATOR

~

You need a way to note the passage of time while you work. You have four basic options:

1. Wear a watch.
2. Put your phone in a dock and set it to display the time.
3. Install a clock on one of the walls in your office.
4. Use the native clock on your computer or laptop.

THE DEVICE you choose doesn't matter as much as its presence in your workspace.

As an aside, I don't recommend using your phone because it'll pose a distraction when you receive texts, phone calls, and various notifications. Nor do I recommend using your computer's clock. It's too easy to disregard. Having said that, if you have no other options, it's better to have *something* with which to track the time than nothing at all.

With a wall clock or wristwatch, you'll be more cognizant of the amount of time it takes to complete tasks. If you set task-specific deadlines (a practice I highly recommend), you'll feel pressure to finish them.

This heightened awareness will sharpen your focus. With the clock in plain view, you'll always know how much remaining time you have available. If you're using a to-do list, you'll also know precisely what you need to get done in that time frame. As the minutes pass, the increasing pressure will spur you to ignore distractions and stay on task.

A lot of people prefer to work without having a way to tell the time. They feel doing so allows them to more easily enter a flow state.

While this may be true for *some* people, I've found that most tend to dawdle when they're unaware of how much time they have at their disposal. It's human nature.

I've seen this in college while observing students and professors. The former would lounge instead of study, and then check their watches and panic when they'd realized how much time had passed. The latter would go off on tangents, and then hurriedly sum things up when they'd realized the class session was ending.

I've witnessed this in Corporate America. Coworkers, confident they had plenty of time, would waste it chatting, checking social media, playing with their phones, and doing anything other than the work they were responsible for. Without a clock or watch to display the time, they managed to convince themselves they had more of it than was actually the case.

Have you ever wondered why grocery stores, shopping malls, and other retail venues lack clocks? Can you recall the last time you saw a clock in a casino? The folks who operate these venues know that if you're aware of the time, you'll be more inclined to hurry. Keeping clocks *off* the walls - essentially, preventing customers from monitoring the time - solves that problem.

Think about that with regard to your workspace. You need a way to monitor the passage of time. I recommend installing a clock on the wall in front of your desk. Ideally, make sure it's in your direct line of sight. You'll find that it'll help you to direct your attention and zero in on the task in front of you.

DRY ERASE BOARD

~

A dry erase board serves two important purposes. First, it allows you to keep track of tasks you need to complete. You can use it as a to-do list, jotting new items down and erasing others as you complete them.

Second, it's a place to record ideas as they come to you. You no longer need to keep the ideas in your head, hoping you'll remember them later. You can jot them down on the board for later evaluation, confident that you'll never lose track of them due to a poor memory.

The jumble of thoughts swimming around in our heads has a devastating effect on our attention and productivity. Each thought poses an open loop that erodes mental clarity. Each one nags us until it's addressed, or recorded and tracked.

When you transfer these thoughts from your head to a dry erase board, you become better able to concentrate. The items are no longer open loops that nag and draw your attention.

Fair warning: not everyone enjoys working with dry erase boards. Some find them cumbersome to write on since the boards are mounted on walls. They prefer to write things down on a pad of paper, or record them online using cloud-based tools, such as EverNote or OneNote.

I suggest you try using a dry erase board. They're relatively inexpensive; many smaller models are available at Amazon for less than $20. If you decide to try it, I recommend investing in several colored markers (these will add $10 to the total cost). Use different colors for different purposes. For example...

- Red for to-do items.
- Blue for appointments and meetings.
- Green for random thoughts.
- Black for brainstorming.

Use the board for at least two weeks. That'll give you enough time to determine whether you enjoy the experience. If you find that you dislike using the board, or that its use fails to help you manage your attention, discard it or give it away. At least you'll know for certain.

Millions of people have incorporated dry erase boards into their workspaces to keep track of tasks, appointments, meetings, and random thoughts. They've found them to be a useful aid with regard to attention management. Try it for yourself. Experiment with this practice over the next two weeks. You may discover a dry erase board is a perfect complement to your office and workflow.

Coming Up Next...

We've just created the perfect work environment. You now need actionable tactics designed to sharpen your focus while you work. In Part III of *Fast Focus*, you'll learn 23 tactics you can start using today.

PART III

---

23 TACTICS THAT WILL IMMEDIATELY IMPROVE YOUR FOCUS

∿

Attention management is tougher than ever these days. Phone calls, emails, and texts conspire against us, working tirelessly to distract us from our work. Meanwhile, the lure of social media, YouTube, and news websites constantly threatens to derail our momentum and break our concentration.

And then there are the distractions created by the people around us. If you work at home, your family may not realize that every interruption cripples your ability to focus. If you're a student, your friends might prefer to goof off rather than study, preventing you from doing the latter. If you work in an office, your coworkers might habitually drop by to chat, unwittingly destroying your concentration in the process.

You need actionable tactics you can rely on to manage your attention in light of these challenges. This section of *Fast Focus* will equip you with everything you need to keep distractions at bay and stay on task.

Let's get started!

TACTIC #1: SET A TIMER

~

I n *Part II: How To Create An Environment That Helps You To Focus*, I advised installing a clock on the wall in front of your desk. A clock in plain view will keep you aware of the time.

You should also have a timer on your desk. Use it to set self-imposed deadlines for individual tasks (or batches of tasks).

For example, suppose you're working on a presentation. You know from experience that you require two hours to complete it. Set your timer for two hours and get to work. The timer, counting down in front of you, will keep you focused. It'll keep you on track, making you less inclined to procrastinate and less suscep-tible to distractions.

Deadlines spur us to take action. A timer is crucial because it provides a visual gauge. Placed on our workstations where we can see the allotted time counting down, it directs our attention to the task at hand. It ensures the task or project we're working on receives the highest immediate priority. We focus on our work rather than procrastinate because we're aware the time we allotted to the task is running out.

A few quick tips:

- Set realistic deadlines. Keep Hofstadter's law in mind: things always take longer than we think. Take into account potential challenges you might face on the road to finishing a task or project.
- Avoid setting deadlines that are too lenient. If you need one hour, don't allot two hours.
- Create a reward-or-consequence system. If you meet your deadline, reward yourself (for example, enjoy a piece of chocolate). If you miss your deadline, deprive yourself of the reward.
- Work in small time chunks. Instead of setting your timer for three hours, set it for an hour at a time (at most). Take 10-minute breaks between each time chunk.

What type of timer should you use? You have three basic options. You can use a kitchen timer, a phone app, or Google. Personally, I prefer to use a digital kitchen timer when I'm working at home. I don't like using my phone because its apps pose too much of a distraction (phones are productivity killers).

I can't use a kitchen timer when I work in coffeeshops (not without distracting other people, at least). So I use Google's native timer. Here's how to activate it...

Open your browser and visit Google. In the search box, type "timer 30 minutes" and hit Enter. Notice that Google will set a timer for 30 minutes. It'll start counting down immediately. When the 30 minutes elapses, the timer will emit a loud beeping sound. The beeping will continue until you turn it off or reset the timer.

Google's timer recognizes hours, minutes, and seconds, and

you can set it for any length of time you desire using those units of measurement. The best part is that it's free and simple to use.

The only drawback (for me, anyway) is that Google's alarm is loud. I'm often startled by it, especially if I've managed to reach a flow state. But that's a small price to pay for the ability to concentrate and stay on task.

One quick note: if you intend to use Google's timer while working in a public venue, I recommend wearing earbuds or headphones. That way, the alarm won't disturb those sitting near you when it goes off.

TACTIC #2: LIMIT THE NUMBER OF
DAILY TASKS TO FIVE

~

The more you have on your plate, the less you'll be able to focus on any single item. As you work on one task, the others will nag at you and demand your attention. Moreover, if you have 10, 15, or an even greater number of tasks on your to-do list, you'll inevitably start to feel stressed. That will further erode your concentration, making you more prone to distraction.

I recommend you limit the number of items on your daily to-do list to five. Five is few enough that you'll be able to focus on them one at a time without the worry of leaving some unfinished. If you know you'll have time to complete every task on your list, you won't feel pestered by the ones waiting for your attention. They'll eventually get addressed as long as you allot sufficient time for them.

I learned this the hard way. Years ago, I used to overestimate how much I could get done during a given time period. Consequently, my to-do lists regularly included far too many tasks. Juggling these tasks caused me great stress. I always felt as if I was playing catchup, watching time slip away while realizing there was no conceivable way I could get everything done.

Given those circumstances, staying focused was impossible. And the quality of my work suffered for it.

When you limit yourself to five tasks per day, you avoid this predicament. You'll feel as if you have a firm handle on everything that appears on your to-do list. You'll not only know exactly what you need to do during the day, but you'll also feel confident that every task will be completed on time.

The result? You'll feel more relaxed, more creative, and be better able to concentrate. Moreover, the quality of your work will improve.

So take the pressure off yourself. Review your daily to-do list and identify all nonessential tasks. Either reschedule them for a later date or get rid of them entirely if they're unnecessary. Then, direct your attention toward completing the five *important* items that remain on your list.

If you finish the five items and have time left over at the end of the day, address the others. Consider it a bonus if you're able to complete any of them. The key is to remove the unimportant and extraneous items from your main to-do list. That'll give you the freedom to zero in on the ones that'll move the needle furthest with regard to your responsibilities and goals.

TACTIC #3: KNOW YOUR REASON

～

Everything we do, from brushing our teeth in the morning to playing with our kids in the evening, is prompted by a reason. We do things with purpose.

When we lack a specific purpose, we become more susceptible to distractions. We focus on whatever our brains tell us to focus on, rather than the other way around. We become passengers rather than drivers.

Imagine trying to work productively as your attention is commandeered by everything around you. How can you possibly concentrate under these circumstances? That's what happens when you work on something without knowing your reason for doing so.

For example, suppose you're a college student and need to study for an exam. You expect to put in four hours of study time in order to feel adequately prepared. That's four hours of *focused* time.

You have an obvious reason to study: the exam will affect your final grade in the class. Therefore, you want to get a high score on it. The only way to do that (besides cheating) is to study.

But suppose you're not thinking of the reason. It's intuitive, and so it escapes your notice. Making matters worse, the drudgery of studying for exams eclipses it. It's difficult to keep your eyes on the prize (a respectable final grade) when you're buried under 40 pages of notes to memorize.

Under these circumstances, you'll find it difficult to concentrate. You'll be distracted by your friends, your phone, and even random strangers walking past you - anything that's unrelated to your schoolwork. Your brain will seek out such distractions to avoid focusing on the monotonous task at hand. It craves gratification and engagement, both for which studying is a poor source.

This is why it's imperative to know your reason for doing something. Purpose is what drives us. It gives us clarity and keeps us on task. It's one of the keys to effectively managing your attention.

It's common to experience internal resistance when you're trying to focus. This resistance materializes when your brain fails to recognize why you're taking action. To squash it and get to work, contemplate your purpose.

For example, if you need to study for a college exam, remind yourself that your performance on the exam will affect your class grade. If you're completing a report for your boss, note that your work will influence his or her business decisions. If you're cleaning your home, remember that you're receiving guests that evening and want to make a good impression.

In short, know your "why." You'll find that it'll focus your attention and help you avoid distractions that would otherwise derail your momentum and cripple your productivity.

TACTIC #4: BEGIN EACH WORK/STUDY SESSION WITH AEROBIC EXERCISE

~

Plenty of studies have shown that exercise reduces the risk of Alzheimer's disease,[1] improves cognitive processing,[2] and boosts memory.[3] Researchers have also found that it improves attention management.[4] People who engage in aerobic exercise are better able to focus afterwards.

The science behind this latter effect involves the hippocampus, the part of the brain responsible for producing new memories. Neurologists believe aerobic exercise increases blood flow to the hippocampus. This elevates the individual's alertness and focus, allowing him or her to devote more "attentional resources" to the task at hand.

How can you wield this science to your advantage? Exercise right before you sit down to work or study.

To be clear, you don't need to visit a gym. Nor do you need to run several miles. Sixty seconds of energetic physical exertion will suffice. Here are a few ideas:

- Do 10 pushups

- Do 10 squats
- Do 10 crunches
- Do 20 jumping jacks
- Do 10 chair dips
- Do a 30-second sprint outside
- Jump rope for 60 seconds
- Shadow box for 60 seconds

The goal is to elevate your heart rate. According to researchers, that'll increase the volume of red blood cells providing oxygen to your brain. Again, it only takes 60 seconds. That's ideal if you're working in short time blocks (e.g. 30-minute sessions).

Researchers have also found that exercise increases the volume of a particular protein responsible for brain growth.[5] The protein is referred to as brain-derived neurotrophic factor, or BDNF. It's believed to contribute to neuron growth and improve synaptic transmission.

The result? Better information processing. Better memory. And improved attention management.

If you need to concentrate, roll up your sleeves and exert yourself. It literally only takes a minute. Increase blood flow to your hippocampus and enjoy the resulting boost in focus.

---

1. https://www.ncbi.nlm.nih.gov/pmc/articles/PMC4005962/
2. https://www.ncbi.nlm.nih.gov/pmc/articles/PMC3768113/
3. http://journal.frontiersin.org/article/10.3389/fnagi.2013.00075/full
4. https://www.ncbi.nlm.nih.gov/pmc/articles/PMC3951958/
5. http://web.stanford.edu/group/hopes/cgi-bin/hopes_test/brain-derived-neurotrophic-factor-bdnf/

TACTIC #5: CAPTURE IDEAS QUICKLY

~

One of the biggest distractions we deal with on a daily basis are our unexpressed thoughts and ideas. They float around in our heads, demanding our attention.

For example, you can probably relate to the following scenario: you're hard at work when you suddenly have a promising idea. You try to ignore it so you can stay on task. But the idea hangs there, in your mind, refusing to go away. Before long, you're researching it online and your current task has been all but forgotten.

It's healthy to have ideas, of course. Creativity is a boon in every context. The problem is, random ideas can destroy your focus if you fail to address them in a productive manner.

Here's the challenge: you don't want to forget your ideas. At the same time, you don't want them to break your concentration and momentum. So how do you address your ideas while maintaining your focus?

I've found that the best approach is to have a way to record them immediately. That way, you can store them for later review without allowing them to pull you away from your work. Here are a few options for recording your ideas so you can stay on task:

- Pen and paper
- Evernote
- OneNote
- Todoist
- Google Keep
- White board
- Chalk board
- Digital voice recorder

When an errant thought crosses your mind, write it down, store it online, or dictate it into a recorder. Don't allow it to float around in your head. Document it and move on.

David Allen, creator of the acclaimed Getting Things Done system, calls such thoughts "open loops." They're intentions that haven't yet been categorized. They represent things we want to do or need to do. Left "open," they nag us and pull at our attention.

Close these open loops. Store these ideas. Otherwise, they'll tax your memory, distract you, and make you more inclined to procrastinate.

Personally, I prefer to use pen and paper for capturing most of my ideas. Having said that, when I suddenly think of *to-do items* that need to be addressed, I record them online using Todoist. And if the ideas are related to pending projects - for example, something I want to include in a book I'm writing - I'll record them in Evernote, where the project details are already stored.

I avoid using my phone to capture ideas. As I mentioned, it poses too much of a distraction. As soon as I pick it up, I'm tempted to visit Facebook, call a friend, and check email. If you have more discipline than I, using your phone may not pose an issue.

You can download the apps for Evernote, Todoist, and

OneNote for free. All three are platform-independent; they're available for the iPhone as well as Android devices.

I work mostly on my Macbook. I use the Chrome browser and have "pinned" tabs open for Evernote and Todoist. (Pinning a tab prevents its accidental closure.) I can capture ideas online (when suitable) in seconds and quickly get back to work.

It's a system I've used for years. I recommend you try it out if you work online and your phone is a constant distraction to you.

TACTIC #6: IDENTIFY TRIGGERS THAT LEAD YOU TO DISTRACTION

~

Most people assume they become distracted out of boredom. With nothing to engage their minds, their attention is drawn toward anything that promises to do so, if only for a moment.

The truth is, distractions are triggered. Internal or external stimuli break our concentration and pull us off task. If you're tired of fighting distractions, it's important to identify what triggers them in the first place.

Let's address internal triggers that can disrupt your focus. Note that some in the following list are physical while others are psychological:

- Food cravings
- Tendency to procrastinate
- Boredom or restlessness
- Frustration
- Pain (e.g. headache, toothache, etc.)
- Moodiness

These stimuli make you more susceptible to distraction. For example, if you have a deep hankering for your favorite candy bar, you'll find it difficult to concentrate on the task at hand. If you're a habitual procrastinator, your brain will find ways to divert your attention elsewhere. Boredom, frustration, pain, and depression will also erode your attention.

If you hope to keep distractions at bay, you must first address these triggers. You must come up with and implement effective ways to avoid or suppress them.

For example, I experience headaches when I eat too much sugary food. These headaches make it difficult to concentrate. If I need to get things done, particularly creative things like writing a book, I either limit my sugar intake or have plenty of ibuprofen available.

What about *external* stimuli that make us more susceptible to distraction? Review the following list and consider how each item has the potential to wrangle your attention away from the task or project you're working on:

- Emails
- Texts
- Phone calls
- Social media
- Television news programs
- The internet
- Noisy co-workers

I'm sure you can relate to at least a few of these items. If you're like me, you relate to all of them. Each one can ruin your concentration, derail your momentum, and severely hamper your productivity.

Here again, it's important to recognize the *reasons* you're distracted. It's only by identifying your personal external triggers that you'll be able to devise practices to avoid them.

Emails used to pose a huge distraction for me. Whenever I check my email - I have several accounts - I'm compelled to be thorough. I read each message and respond when doing so is appropriate. This can take a significant amount of time.

I used to keep a browser tab open to Gmail. Without fail, new messages would draw my attention as soon as they arrived. They would distract me to the point that I couldn't concentrate unless I dealt with them.

Today, I check email twice per day. The first check happens around noon; the second happens around 5:00 p.m. I no longer keep a browser tab open to Gmail. Nor do I keep my phone near me while I work. Thus, I'm no longer notified of - and distracted by - new emails the moment they arrive.

Identify your personal triggers for distraction - both internal and external - and address them in a similar manner. Think of practices you can incorporate into your routine that'll quash them, or at least suppress their effect on you. (For example, I stay away from sugary foods to avoid headaches.) It'll help you to master your attention and stay on task when doing so is important.

TACTIC #7: USE A DAILY TO-DO LIST

❧

One of the purposes of using a to-do list is to record every task, project, or item that needs to be addressed at some point. It allows you to get them out of your head, where they pose open loops. In doing so, you're better able to focus and zero in on the work in front of you.

This effect is related to something known in the psychology field as the Zeigarnik effect. The Zeigarnik effect asserts that unfinished tasks draw our attention more than finished tasks. The former are open loops. When these uncompleted tasks remain in our heads, they pose intrusive thoughts that distract us and hobble our concentration.

Using a to-do list resolves this problem. By recording every task and thought, you can effectively purge them from your short-term memory, where they would otherwise form open loops. By putting them on your list, you can close the loops and stay on task without concern that you'll forget them.

To-do lists serve another purpose that aids attention management: they remind us of all the things we need to do during a given day, or for a particular project.

For example, suppose you're working on a project that involves dozens of individual actions. If these actions are recorded on a list, you don't have to worry about forgetting any of them. You can simply work down your list, crossing items off as you complete them. If these actions were to remain in your head, they'd pose open loops, distracting you from the task at hand. Worse, there's an ever-present risk of neglecting one or more of them. That, too, is likely to pose a distraction.

Once you remove these items from your prefrontal cortex, the area of your brain that handles short-term memory, you'll be better able to focus on the task in front of you. The open loops will no longer distract you. You'll have closed them.

The medium you use to record tasks is less important than the act of recording them. Here are your basic options:

- Paper and pen
- Cloud-based tools (Todoist, Evernote, OneNote, etc.)
- Dry erase board

If you own a tablet that supports note taking with a stylus, you can also use that. The important point is that you find a medium you're comfortable working in.

I use a combination of paper and pen, Todoist, and Evernote. Paper and pen works well for recording random thoughts I don't want to forget, but still need to categorize. I can quickly remove them from my brain and put them aside to attend to them later.

Todoist is my favorite to-do list tool. It offers plenty of flexibility without burying you in useless bells and whistles. I use it to maintain dozens of lists. I can color code them, as well as the individual tasks they contain, according to priority and context. If you've never tried Todoist, I highly recommend it (you can find it at Todoist.com). There's a free version, which will probably suit your needs, and a paid version that offers a ton of bells and whis-tles. I use the free version, and it's more than enough for me.

I find that Evernote is perfect for organizing projects with a bird's-eye view. For example, when I form an idea for a new book, I create a skeleton outline for it in Evernote. I flesh out the outline over the following weeks.

The project - a new book in this example - is still in its early stages while it's in Evernote. It's not yet at the point where I need to focus on individual tasks, such as researching new concepts, perusing scientific journals, writing each section, editing, outsourcing cover creation, etc. Once I'm ready to focus on these tasks, I move the project from Evernote to Todoist.

That's my system. It has proved invaluable for helping me to manage my attention and work productively. If you're looking for a system that'll help you organize and manage multiple projects, I recommend that you try mine. I'm willing to bet you'll have a similarly positive experience.

TACTIC #8: PLAY MUSIC THAT HELPS YOU TO ENTER A FLOW STATE

~

Music serves two purposes when you're trying to concentrate: it drowns out environmental noise and it can help you to enter a flow state.

As I noted in *Part II: How To Create An Environment That Helps You To Focus*, noise in your immediate surroundings can make it difficult to manage your attention. The *type* of noise depends on your environment.

In an office setting, conversation between coworkers can pose a distraction. In a coffee shop, the making of lattes, cappuccino, and the latest sugar-laden "coffee" drinks (e.g. white chocolate mocha with whip cream and a shot a caramel) can be as distracting as a jackhammer. At home, the sound of your kids' favorite television program from the adjoining room can easily divert your attention and ruin your concentration.

Music can help nullify this type of noise. It can drown it out, or at least push it into the background, so that it's no longer a problem.

Note that even silence can be a distraction. Many people are unable to focus without some type of ambient noise. For them, music can replace the silence and help them to concentrate.

Music can help you to reach a state of such sharpened focus that everything around you recedes into the background. This state of mind, referred to as "being in the zone," boosts performance. Researchers have found this to be the case with musicians,[1] athletes,[2][3] and even those who play video games.[4]

The key is the type of music you listen to.

Most people find they're better able to concentrate when they listen to instrumental music. Music with lyrics proves to be too much of a distraction.

Having said that, it's worth noting that *some* people are able to concentrate while listening to select songs *with* lyrics. They're so familiar with their favorite songs that they fade into the background and don't pose a distraction. Personally, I've tried to make this work and failed miserably. But I encourage you to try it yourself.

Not all instrumental music is ideal for helping you to manage your attention. For example, I enjoy listening to rock guitar music (Joe Satriani, Tony MacAlpine, etc.) during my leisure time. But I can't focus while doing so. Invariably, I start tapping my foot and bobbing my head. I might even sway back and forth with the rhythm of the music, drawing stares from those around me if I'm working in coffee shops.

I recommend classical music. While its effectiveness isn't universal, it works for most people. Research shows that baroque music, in particular, is helpful thanks to its uptempo rhythm. It improves the listener's mood, which has a positive effect on his or her concentration and productivity.[5]

I've found that listening to the same classical piece over and over helps me to concentrate and "get in the zone." For example, when I write, I listen to Chopin's Prelude in E minor, Op. 28, No. 4. It plays in a loop in the background. I'm so familiar with it that it has an almost hypnotic effect on me. My brain immediately focuses when it hears the first few notes.

You can find similar classical pieces, namely piano sonatas, nocturnes, and etudes, recorded to play in loops - over and over for 60 minutes - on YouTube. I downloaded Chopin's Prelude in E minor, Op. 28, No. 4 to my Macbook Air. But you can also find the following pieces:

- Beethoven's Für Elise
- Beethoven's Moonlight Sonata
- Chopin's Nocturne Op. 9, No. 2
- Erik Satie's Gnossienne No. 1
- Franz Liszt's La campanella

That's just a sample. You'll find many others on YouTube. I recommend trying each of them and seeing which ones work best for you. I've found that my brain responds best to Chopin's Prelude in E minor, Op. 28, No. 4. But your brain might respond more favorably to Beethoven, Satie, or Liszt.

The takeaway is that the right type of music can sharpen your focus and help you stay on task when other noises in your environment threaten to distract you.

---

1. Richard Parncutt, *The Science and Psychology of Music Performance* (Oxford University Press, 2002)
2. https://www.pbs.org/newshour/science/can-music-make-you-a-better-athlete
3. Steve King, *Running in the Zone* (Trafford Publishing, 2006)
4. https://archive.org/stream/byte-magazine-1981-12/1981_12_BYTE_06-12_Computer_Games#page/n279/mode/2up
5. https://www.sciencedaily.com/releases/2009/04/090423132615.htm

TACTIC #9: TAKE FREQUENT BREAKS

~

Science claims that taking short breaks keep us focused and on task.[1] That makes sense. You've no doubt experienced your own attention waning over long periods of work or study. Our brains are simply not designed to focus for hours on end without rest.

Working without breaks leads to boredom. This makes us more vulnerable to distractions, which, in turn, weakens our ability to concentrate.

When we take frequent breaks, our brains are better able to process new information, form new connections, and commit important details to memory. We also return to our work feeling refreshed, which makes it easier to manage our attention and fight distractions.

Many people choose not to take breaks because they feel guilty doing so. They feel that setting aside work to relax would waste time - time that could be used to get more things done. The irony is that working without rest produces the precise outcome they're trying to avoid. Without rest, their minds become less efficient, they make more mistakes, and become less productive. These consequences force them to spend more time than necessary completing tasks.

Let's assume you're convinced that taking regular and frequent breaks is important, but you're uncertain how to incorporate them into your workday. Here are a few ideas:

- **Work in time chunks.** One popular method is the Pomodoro Technique: work for 25 minutes and take a 5-minute break. Or you might prefer the 52+17 strategy: work for 52 minutes and take a 17-minute break. Experiment to find a work/break interval that complements your workflow.
- **Monitor your attention level.** This requires self-awareness. When you feel your focus beginning to wane, immediately stop working and take a break. Stand up and stretch. Grab a healthy snack (an apple, a few almonds, etc.). Drink a glass of water. Do something - anything! - that interrupts your work session and gives your brain a short, but much-needed respite.
- **Schedule power naps.** Power naps are short. They last between 10 and 30 minutes. On the shorter end, they're essentially an excuse to close your eyes and relax (you're not trying to reach REM sleep). Organize your afternoon into 45 minute time chunks. Schedule 10-minute power naps between them. If you're like me, you'll look forward to these moments when you can put your head back, close your eyes, and ignore everything around you.
- **"Socialize" your breaks.** Call friends and loved ones during your breaks. If you're a naturally-social person, you'll look forward to making these calls. They can serve as incentives to focus on your work without

distraction. You reward yourself by connecting with people you love and value.

- **"Gamify" your breaks.** The underlying idea here is the same as the idea behind socializing your breaks. But rather than calling a friend or loved one, you use your breaks to play your favorite games. I enjoy playing Quell and Space Invaders. You might prefer something entirely different, such as Entanglement[2] or Slither[3].

Give these ideas a try. Or come up with your own. The important thing is that you find a way to incorporate frequent breaks into your workday. Give your brain time to relax between work sessions and you'll experience a greater ability to concentrate when it counts.

---

1. https://www.sciencedaily.com/releases/2011/02/110208131529.htm
2. http://entanglement.gopherwoodstudios.com/
3. http://slither.io/

TACTIC #10: TAKE SHORT WALKS

~

This tactic may sound pedestrian. But it's more helpful than you might think with regard to attention management. Not only does taking a walk give your brain a chance to relax, but there's something about the fresh air that's restorative. It repairs mental fatigue, which can otherwise hamper your ability to fight distractions.

Science agrees. Studies show that taking walks can improve both your focus and short-term memory. The effect is particularly strong when these walks are taken in a natural environment, such as a forest or arboretum.[1] [2] Even the simple act of looking at pictures of nature can have a restorative effect.[3] Attention spans among one study's participants lengthened by as much as 20 percent.

You can probably relate to this from experience. Recall the last time you enjoyed a walk outside, away from your work. The walk probably lifted your mood and helped you to feel more relaxed. Your energy level likely rose. Your mind probably wandered, seeking creative solutions to existing problems.

And when you returned to your work, didn't you feel mentally refreshed? Weren't you better able to concentrate on the task at hand? You may have even noticed that your performance improved; you made fewer mistakes and produced higher-quality work.

These effects are common after taking short walks.

You don't need access to a forest or arboretum to enjoy the cognitive benefits of walking. A walk in any environment can prove helpful. Of course, the attentional benefits of walking in nature will always exceed those of walking on a crowded sidewalk with the constant blare of street traffic in the background. But as with everything in life, work with what you have.

The most common challenge people face is actually *taking* the walks. Many folks are inclined to simply remain at their desks, or worse continue working. They figure that doing so is less hassle. By comparison, pausing their work, getting up, putting on a jacket, telling others where they'll be and for how long, and finally going outside seems like a nuisance. It's easier to take breaks at their desks.

But realize that doing this robs you of the cognitive benefits of walking. You'll miss out on its relaxing, restorative effect. And most importantly, you won't experience the sharpened focus that comes with taking brisk walks outside.

Your attention needs to be reset periodically throughout the day. That's the surest way to stay focused and on task when it counts. Don't just surf the internet at your desk. Don't merely chat with your friends. Get up and go outside. Enjoy the fresh air. You'll not only feel refreshed, but you'll also be better able to concentrate when you need to.

---

1. https://www.ncbi.nlm.nih.gov/pmc/articles/PMC3393816/
2. http://pss.sagepub.com/content/19/12/1207
3. http://www.sciencedirect.com/science/article/pii/S0272494405000381

TACTIC #11: COMMIT TO SINGLE-TASKING

∼

Most people are impressed by the ability to multitask. The capacity for managing several tasks simultaneously seems remarkable to us. We value it. We praise it. Many of us try to develop that faculty in ourselves.

But here's the dirty little secret about multitasking: it doesn't work. Researchers have found that trying to do many things at once makes us more prone to distraction.[1] These distractions impair our performance.

It's easy to understand the nature of this effect. Our brains don't actually attend to multiple tasks at once, even if it seems as if they do. Rather, our brains attend to one task and then another, and then another. When we attend to multiple tasks at the same time, our brains move back and forth between them. This is known as task switching.

Task switching imposes severe attentional costs.[2] First, it requires that multiple tasks remain unfinished. As noted earlier, these unfinished tasks are open loops that distract your attention.

Second, our work quality diminishes and error rate increases with the number and complexity of the tasks we try to juggle. This has a profoundly negative impact on our productivity.

Think about a friend or family member who's a habitual multitasker. Have you ever tried to have a substantive conversation with this individual while he or she was juggling multiple tasks? You likely found the experience frustrating. The individual probably had a difficult time focusing on the conversation, and was thereby unable to contribute to it in a meaningful way.

This is the result of task switching. It cripples concentration.

You can immediately improve your focus by committing to *single*-tasking. Attend to one task at a time. Resist the temptation to address other items while you work on that task.

Fair warning: this won't be easy if you're a habitual multitasker. But rest assured, with time, diligence, and consistent application, you can train yourself to hone in on a single task while ignoring all others.

I know firsthand the struggles of abandoning multitasking and committing to a single-tasking habit. Years ago, I used to pride myself on my "ability" to juggle numerous tasks. I'd talk on the phone with my parents while working on spreadsheets, reading the news, and checking my latest sales numbers. I'd watch television while reading a book and checking email. I'd shave and talk to friends on the phone while driving.

In retrospect, I realize that my performance suffered greatly across the spectrum of tasks I was juggling. For example, if I was reading and watching TV at the same time, I was often unable to recall the story elements of both the book and television program. If I was shaving while driving, I was likely to leave behind patches of stubble (and likely to veer into other lanes). If I was talking on the phone while reviewing spreadsheets, I was a poor conversationalist.

These problems stemmed from a lack of focus borne from multitasking.

Over the years, I trained myself to attend to one task at a time.

But I admit, it was a long, difficult, and frustrating journey. In the beginning, I couldn't focus for more than two or three minutes without being distracted. I was an absentminded mess. And I beat myself up each time my attention was commandeered by a distraction.

I eventually learned to forgive myself for such failures. That was the only way to get back on track. The effort was worthwhile. For me, the ability to single-task has been one of the most important steps toward managing my attention.

I strongly recommend adopting this habit into your own work process if you haven't already done so. You'll find that it improves your focus, raises the quality of your work, and increases your productivity along the way.

---

1. http://www.pnas.org/content/106/37/15583.full
2. http://www.apa.org/research/action/multitask.aspx

TACTIC #12: BATCH PROCESS SIMILAR TASKS

❧

atch processing is usually thought of in the context of computing. A computer executes a series of programs or jobs without needing manual intervention for each one. The programs and jobs are typically queued during the day and then prompted to execute at day's end.

One advantage of batch processing (again, in the context of computing) is that it puts less load on the computer's processor and cores. Another is that it doesn't require intervention for each job. No one needs to remain near the computer to prompt it to execute the queued programs.

Your brain can work in a similar manner. Learn to leverage this attentional attribute and you'll experience increased focus and productivity. Here's how you can use batch processing to your advantage.

First, think about everything you need to do today. Write down each item (or record them online using Todoist, OneNote, or Evernote). You need to see them displayed in front of you.

Second, review your list and look for tasks that are similar to one another. Group them together. Here are a few examples:

- Emails you need to read and respond to
- Blog posts you need to write
- Bills you need to pay
- Phone calls you need to make
- Appointments and meetings you need to schedule
- Reports you need to complete
- Chores you need to perform

Third, schedule a chunk of time (for example, 20 minutes) on your daily calendar for each group. Use that time to address only those items.

By doing the above, you're prompting your brain to batch process tasks. The advantage is that because these tasks are similar, addressing them will require fewer cognitive resources. Your brain won't need to be prompted to perform each one since it'll know intuitively what to do next.

For example, suppose you're paying bills. It's something you've done every month for years. As such, your brain is familiar with the process and can execute a series of known "jobs" to complete the batch.

For each bill, it'll know to look at the amount owed, write a check, and record the details for your records. Your brain can perform these actions without requiring significant cognitive or attentional resources. It'll execute each job, one after the next, over and over, until all of the jobs in the batch have been completed. The task is made easier because the tasks (or jobs) are similar. As a result, your brain can more easily focus on getting through the batch.

Batch processing will also help you to sidestep the attentional costs that accompany task switching (we discussed these costs in the previous section). Imagine yourself paying a bill, then working on a report for a few minutes, and then making a phone call. After completing the call, you send an email, read a memo, clear off your workspace, schedule a meeting, and pay another bill. This is known as *transaction* processing. Every task requires your attention.

Transaction processing imposes significant task switching costs on your attention. It not only takes more time, but it also impairs your ability to concentrate. Moreover, it makes you more receptive to distractions.

You're able to avoid these effects when you *batch* process. You'll stay mentally sharp for longer periods. That'll help you to maintain your focus, fight distractions, and stay on task.

Consider how this tactic can affect your productivity. In the section *Top 10 Obstacles To Staying Focused*, I noted that your brain needs 20 minutes to get back on track following an interruption. When you attend to tasks in batches, you minimize transactional interruptions. The result? It becomes easier to achieve a flow state in which your productivity soars!

It's worth noting that batch processing is most effective with tasks that require minimal creative thought or critical thinking. Answering emails fits the bill. So does scheduling meetings, paying bills, and performing household chores. Doing complex math problems, creating elaborate systems, and performing deep research, all of which require substantial cognitive resources, are less suited to batching.

But for mundane tasks, it's a great way to manage your attention and boost your productivity in the process.

TACTIC #13: ARRANGE YOUR DAY INTO TIME CHUNKS

~

Some people call it time blocking. Others refer to it as the Pomodoro Technique (although the Pomodoro Technique is a very restrictive approach). Still others call it time chunking.

Whatever you prefer to call it, here are the basic steps:

1. You designate a specific amount of time to address a specific task.
2. You spend that time working only on that task.

The amount of time you allot for a given chunk or block might be 10 minutes or five hours (or more). Much depends on the task - or tasks if you're batch processing - that you intend to address during that time period.

Arranging your day into time chunks offers three advantages:

1. **It makes you more productive.** Allotting a set period of time assigns a deadline for the task. As Parkinson's

law states, "work expands so as to fill the time available for its completion." Setting a deadline effectively shortens the time you'll spend working on the task.

2. **It makes you feel more relaxed.** You'll no longer feel stressed about whether you'll have sufficient time to complete everything on your to-do list. Your schedule will be filled with time chunks designated to work on your to-do items. Emergencies notwithstanding, that eliminates the mystery of how your day will progress.

3. **It sharpens your focus.** The chunk of time you allot for a specific item keeps you on task. You'll know from the start that your attention should be devoted solely to the task in front of you. You won't be tempted to work on other things, and suffer the attendant attentional costs, during that time chunk.

How do you arrange your day into time chunks? First, it helps to have an idea of how much time you need to complete specific tasks. This knowledge will allow you to assign chunks that spur you to action without giving you too much time (remember Parkinson's law).

Second, once you've assigned time chunks for all of the tasks on your to-do list, put them on your calendar. Doing so blocks off the time so you won't double-book your schedule. I prefer Google Calendar. It's effective and simple to use. It's also free.

Third, if a time chunk is longer than 45 minutes, plan to take at least one break. Schedule multiple breaks if it spans longer than 90 minutes.

For example, suppose you've planned a three-hour time chunk to work on an important presentation. Here's how you might schedule your breaks:

- Work for 45 minutes.

- Take a 10-minute break.
- Work for 45 minutes.
- Take a 15-minute break.
- Work for 45 minutes.
- Take a 20-minute break.

Notice how the duration of the breaks increases after each 45-minute work session. This is because staying focused for 45 minutes is hard work. It's mentally taxing. To stay fresh, you need to give your brain sufficient time to relax, especially if your work required deep concentration.

By the time you finish your third and longest break, you'll feel refreshed, focused, and ready to start your next time chunk.

TACTIC #14: DISCONNECT

~

I f you're like most people, your phone and the internet are the two largest distractions threatening your focus. Together, they can make it nearly impossible for you to stay on task and get things done.

Your phone gives you instant and continuous access to texts, emails, and social media. Each new message produces an audible alert (assuming you have your phone notifications turned on). These alerts are distractions. They disrupt your concentration, even if you manage to ignore your phone after they sound.

The internet is even worse. A single search on Google can lead you down a rabbit hole that consumes hours of valuable time. Worse, the "sound bite" nature of online engagement - from quick Google searches and snarky Facebook posts to 140-character "tweets" - has shortened our attention spans. Researchers claim goldfish are now able to focus for longer periods than humans.[1]

The solution is simplicity itself: disconnect while you work. Turn off your phone (we'll cover this in more detail later). Disengage your Wi-Fi connection. In short, eliminate these potential distractions at the outset.

When you're ready to take a break, feel free to grab your phone and reconnect to the internet. (Or better yet, leave your phone on your desk and go for a brisk walk outside.) Read and respond to missed texts, check your email, and visit Facebook. Check out the most recent news headlines and watch the latest funny videos on YouTube. But when your break is over, sever the connections and get back to work.

If you need to look something up online related to the task your working on, make a note of it and keep working. Research the item later rather than breaking your momentum.

You'll find that when you disconnect, you'll feel less stressed, more relaxed, and better able to concentrate. You'll be far less susceptible to distractions, not only to new texts, emails, and social media updates, but also disturbances in your immediate working environment (e.g. loud coworkers, noisy copy machines, etc.).

Disconnecting from your phone and the internet allows your brain to focus its attention on what matters, ignoring everything else in the process.

---

1. http://www.nytimes.com/2016/01/22/opinion/the-eight-second-attention-span.html

TACTIC #15: LIMIT THE TIME YOU SPEND IN MEETINGS

~

W hen I worked in Corporate America, nothing grated on my nerves so much as meetings. I seethed every time I saw a meeting on my schedule. It meant that block of time was lost to me.

It wasn't that I thought meetings were unnecessary. On the contrary, the projects I was involved in required getting together with other contributors. We needed to keep the group updated on our respective progress and oftentimes collaborate to resolve shared challenges.

My aversion to meetings stemmed from the amount of time they sucked out of my schedule. Few lasted less than an hour. Most went on longer.

I can count on one hand the number of times the latter was necessary. On most occasions, meetings went long because everyone was seated and comfortable. Worse, food was often provided. There was little incentive to expedite things.

Over time, I used a tactic that helped me to avoid overly-long meetings. When someone wanted to discuss something with me and suggested scheduling a meeting to do so, I countered by suggesting we discuss the matter at that moment - preferably while standing.

I found that, in most cases, the topic that needed discussion didn't require an hour. It didn't even require 30 minutes. Ten minutes was usually sufficient. Often, five minutes sufficed. As Sir Richard Branson once said...

 "It's very rare that a meeting on a single topic should need to last more than five to 10 minutes."

Clearing my schedule of meetings produced numerous benefits. For one thing, I could devote myself to work that required deep thought and concentration. Without interrupting my work to attend an unnecessary meeting, I could more easily achieve a flow state. This allowed me to better focus on whatever task was on my desk, and build momentum toward its completion.

Think about your typical day. Is a large portion of it spent in meetings? Do you wish you could reclaim that time for more productive use? Are you tired of having to set your work aside, severing your concentration, to attend meetings you know will yield little value?

If so, here's what I recommend:

- When someone asks to meet with you (presumably for at least an hour, and possibly longer), suggest an impromptu meeting at that moment.
- If you must attend a meeting, suggest it be conducted while standing.
- If possible, avoid meetings where food is available. Food leads to comfort, which quells the incentive to hurry.
- If you're the one responsible for scheduling a meeting, allocate a smaller-than-usual window of time for it.

For example, rather than scheduling an hour-long meeting, schedule it for 15 minutes.

- Avoid attending meetings with more than 10 participants.
- Ask that meetings remain focused on the stated agenda.
- Ask that all meetings be scheduled after lunch. Most people experience a heightened level of focus and productivity during the morning hours. Block off that valuable time for your own work.

Spending less time in meetings allows you to spend more time on your own tasks and projects. But the *bigger* advantage is that it leaves you free to work in a focused state. You won't need to disrupt your workflow arbitrarily to attend low-value meetings that hobble your momentum and ruin your productivity.

The result? You'll be better able to manage your attention and fight distractions as you attend to the high-priority, high-value tasks on your to-do list.

TACTIC #16: RESET OTHERS' EXPECTATIONS

~

N o one cares more about your time and focus than you. No one else will take responsibility for it. So it's up to you to set others' expectations.

If you want to avoid the trap of a reactive workflow - where you're constantly catering to others' impromptu demands - you must set rules concerning your availability. Then, you must explain those rules to the people most likely to disrupt your work. Otherwise, you'll always be vulnerable to interruptions and prevented from achieving true focus. You can expect your productivity and work quality to plummet as a result.

The first step is to identify the most common circumstances that interrupt your workflow. Here are a few possibilities:

- Coworkers visit your office to chat or ask for help
- If you work at home, people drop by unannounced, expecting you to invite them in and entertain them
- Friends and family members call you on the phone, expecting you to take their calls

- Coworkers email you and expect a response within the hour
- Friends text you and expect a response within minutes

It's likely the most burdensome expectations - those that have the biggest impact on your focus and productivity - come from a select few people in your life. With that in mind, the second step is to make a list of the top five offenders.

Think about the coworker who regularly drops by your office to chat. Think of the family member who's often irritated that you don't immediately return his or her calls and emails. Think of the friend who sends you dozens of texts per day, and expects you to promptly respond to each of them. Think of the neighbor who regularly drops by unannounced because he knows you're home (and doesn't realize you're working).

You can probably count the worst offenders on one hand.

The third step is to brainstorm a way to reset their expectations.

When I went through this process years ago, I took a draconian approach. My doing so was an emotional reaction to a mounting wave of interruptions combined with increased stress. I couldn't get anything done, felt enormous pressure, and consequently developed a short fuse. Eventually, I went off like a lit powder keg.

I don't recommend taking that approach. It's a surefire recipe for hurt feelings and damaged relationships.

Instead, think of a diplomatic way to approach each of the top offenders you identified in Step 2. For example, suppose you're trying to reset the expectations of a coworker who keeps dropping by your office to chat. You might try the following approach:

 "Sam, I'd love to chat with you. But the morning hours are when I'm at my most productive. Are you able to come back at 1:00 p.m.?"

With this response, you're making Sam feel important, but also clearly communicating that you're not available to chat. Plus, you control the time of the interruption by suggesting he come back at 1:00 p.m. That's immediately following lunch when your focus is likely to be at a low level anyway.

Don't be afraid to reset others' expectations. Remember, they won't do it on their own. And don't let your frustration build up to the point that you react like a lit powder keg. Approach the top offenders with civility and diplomacy, and you may be surprised by how receptive they are to the feedback.

TACTIC #17: TURN YOUR PHONE OFF

~

Your phone may be ruining your concentration. It can do so even if you refuse to answer it when it beeps, chirps, rings, or vibrates.

Researchers reported evidence of this effect in 2015 in the *Journal of Experimental Psychology: Human Perception and Performance*.[1] They monitored the performance of 212 undergraduate students at Florida State University. The students were put into three groups: those who received calls, those who received texts, and those who received no phone notifications whatsoever. They found the following:

> "Cellular phone notifications alone significantly disrupted performance on an attention-demanding task, even when participants did not directly interact with a mobile device during the task."

You've experienced the effect firsthand. Calls and texts that are irrelevant to your work break your concentration. Importantly, it's not just the act of reaching for your phone that does so. Even the *sound* of your phone is a distraction. Its notifications pull at your attention, nagging you until you check them.

For this reason, I strongly recommend you turn your phone off while you work. You'll be better able to focus. You'll find it easier to fight other distractions. You'll also avoid seeing the app badges alerting you to five new voicemails, 78 new emails, and 31 new text messages. And importantly, you'll sidestep the time trap of checking social media.

Instead, without your phone to distract you, you'll be able to concentrate on your work. You'll become more productive, make fewer errors, and feel more relaxed in the process. You'll also end up feeling happier because you've been able to get more things done or attend to deeper, more attention-demanding work.

What if you're addicted to your phone? There's a simple solution. Numerous apps have been designed to help you control the addiction. These apps allow you to designate a period of time during which they block other apps of your choosing.

For example, you can block your social media and texting apps for two hours. Some of these tools can even disable your phone's internet access for a select period of time.

Use of these tools mitigates the risk of your phone's notifications busting your concentration and tearing you away from your work. They're ideal for the phone addict.

Here are a few such tools that have received high marks from users:

- Forest (iOS, Android)
- BreakFree (iOS, Android)
- Offtime (iOS, Android)
- AppDetox (Android)
- Moment (iOS)

Personally, I turn my phone off while I work. It's a simpler solution. I've found that keeping it turned off does more than just sharpen my focus and boost my productivity. It has also helped me to reset others' expectations regarding when I'm likely to return their calls and respond to their emails (I don't text).

Try it for yourself. The next time you need to concentrate, turn off your phone. You'll find that you're more focused. If you're like me, you'll also be happier, more relaxed, and in a better mood.

---

1. https://www.ncbi.nlm.nih.gov/pubmed/26121498

TACTIC #18: MANAGE YOUR ENERGY LEVELS

~

Our energy levels fluctuate throughout the day. We're more focused and productive during periods of high energy. We're less focused and more prone to distraction during periods of low energy. The trick is to identify these periods and organize your workflow to make the best use of them.

I recommend a simple three-step process.

The **first step** is to create a spreadsheet. Google Sheets is ideal because it's free and you can access your data from any computer, phone, or tablet. Use the leftmost column to designate the time of day in 15-minute increments. Start with the time you wake up in the morning and end with the time you go to bed in the evening.

Title the next column "Energy Level." Here, you'll record your energy level at various times of the day. Use values between one and five, with "one" signifying high energy and "five" signifying low energy.

Title the next column "Notes." Here, you'll record details that may be relevant to your fluctuating energy levels. For example, you might jot down in the 8:15 a.m. row that you ate breakfast, and note the foods you ate. These details will prove useful for later review.

The **second step** is to track your energy levels over the next two weeks. Input values between one and five into your spreadsheet to indicate your energy at various points of the day. The frequency and time is entirely up to you. When I did this for myself, I recorded my energy levels at the following times:

- 8:00 a.m. (following coffee)
- 10:00 a.m. (following breakfast)
- 12:00 p.m. (preceding lunch)
- 1:30 p.m. (following lunch)
- 3:00 p.m. (afternoon slump)
- 5:00 p.m. (end of the workday)
- 7:00 p.m. (following dinner)
- 10:30 p.m. (near bedtime)

Notice that the times were near events that were likely to influence my energy levels. For example, I wanted to monitor how breakfast affected my energy, and so recorded the latter at 10:00 a.m. This is roughly 30 minutes after eating.

I found it helpful to record specifics in the "Notes" column of my spreadsheet. For example, I recorded whether I had a heavy lunch (pasta) or a healthy one (chicken salad). If I went for a brisk walk at 2:30 p.m., I recorded that detail in the 3:00 p.m. row. This gave me information that I could then use to better manage my energy throughout the day.

The **third step** comes at the end of the two-week tracking period. That's when it's time to review your spreadsheet. Peruse each day and look for trends. Note times of the day when your energy levels are low. Note when they're high.

I found that my energy plummeted around 3:00 p.m., and I

received a second wind around 5:00 p.m. I also found that unhealthy foods - a donut for breakfast, a candy bar after lunch, etc. - had a measurably negative impact on my energy. In contrast, short bursts of exercise - a 5-minute walk outside, 10 pushups, etc. - had a measurably *positive* impact.

Once you've identified your low-energy and high-energy times of day, adjust your workflow to complement them. Schedule "deep work" - the type of work that requires considerable focus - during high-energy periods. Schedule easy work - for example, responding to emails, returning phone calls, and scheduling meetings - during low-energy periods.

Also, look for changes you can make that'll help you to further leverage high-energy periods. For example, after examining my spreadsheet, I quickly discovered that junk food was severely detrimental to my energy levels. It impaired my ability to concentrate, made me more susceptible to distractions, and made me lethargic.

The takeaway is that your energy levels dictate the extent to which you're able to focus. The problem is, you can't maintain high energy throughout the entire day. Our brains aren't wired that way.

The solution is to track your fluctuating energy levels on a spreadsheet, and use the information to adjust your workflow accordingly.

TACTIC #19: MEDITATE

~

I t shouldn't be a surprise that meditation improves your focus. It's an effective way to reclaim a sense of inner calm. It's a tool for purging the stresses and distractions that burden you, and being present in the moment.

Researchers have found that meditation offers attentional benefits. In 2007, the journal *Proceedings of the National Academy of Sciences* published a study following a group of 40 Chinese college students.[1] The authors found that time spent in meditation lead to marked improvement in their ability to concentrate.

Meditation doesn't require that you light candles or burn incense. Nor do you need to sit with your legs crossed and mutter "Ohmmmmm" over and over.

I mention this because many people have the wrong idea about meditation. They imagine robed, bald monks sitting in cavernous temples with their eyes closed, legs crossed, and their thumbs and index fingers delicately touching. That has become the representative image of the practice in their minds. It's no wonder so many people are turned off by it!

In truth, meditation comes in many forms. Some are so simple that you can do them anywhere, as long as you have peace and quiet. Moreover, some variants only take a few minutes to perform. That's useful if you're limited on time.

I practice mindful meditation. It's a simple form that involves relaxing and focusing on your breathing. I set a timer for three minutes, and close my eyes. Then, I take slow, deep breaths. I concentrate on each inhalation and exhalation, and ignore all other thoughts.

I usually do this at my desk. But you can do it anywhere, as long as it's peaceful. You can sit or stand. It's your choice. You can keep your eyes open if that's your preference. If you do so, I recommend that you fix your eyes on a single object in your immediate environment - for example, a book if you're in your office or a tree if you're sitting at the park.

You only need to do this for a few minutes to feel relaxed, refreshed, and refocused.

As I mentioned, there are many types of meditation. But if you've never tried it, I recommend starting with the simplest form: mindful meditation, the type I practice. Set a timer for three minutes, close your eyes, and concentrate on your breathing. You may be stunned at the extent to which this simple exercise can sharpen your focus.

---

1. http://www.pnas.org/content/104/43/17152.full

TACTIC #20: AVOID YOUR EMAIL

~

O ne of the problems with email is that checking it seems harmless. We tell ourselves it'll only take a few minutes. Most of us know better from experience, but that doesn't stop our brains from convincing us otherwise. So we log into Gmail, Outlook, or Yahoo with the best of intentions, and predictably end up spending far more time than we planned.

Another problem with email is that it's a major distraction. You know this from experience. If you work with a browser tab open to your email program, you know how irresistible new messages are. You want to find out who sent them and what they regard. You know you should stay on task, but your brain convinces you that someone might need an immediate response. So you check your email and fall down the proverbial rabbit hole.

There's another problem with having your email program open while you work: it agitates the fear of missing out (FOMO). This is the same fear that prompts us to check our phones the moment a new text arrives. We don't want to miss an opportunity, whether it's to engage with a friend, participate in the latest gossip, or enjoy a new internet meme. FOMO is one of the biggest reasons new emails draw our attention. Unfortunately, succumbing to the temptation destroys our focus.

I recommend that you avoid your email, at least for most of the day. Don't keep a browser tab open to Gmail (or whatever email platform you use). Don't check email whenever the mood strikes. Don't check just to see if you received a response to an email you sent earlier.

Pick two times of the day to check your email. Try to pick times that cater to your energy levels and workflow productivity.

For example, I currently check email each day around noon and at 5:00 p.m. I actively avoid checking it in the morning hours. It's too easy to get trapped in it and spend too much time reading and responding to messages. Plus, my energy levels are at their highest point in the morning hours. I don't want to waste that time on a noncritical task.

I check and respond to emails at noon while I eat lunch, and again at 5:00 p.m. when I'm winding down for the day.

You may have a completely different schedule based on your personal energy levels and your obligations at work and home. I recommend using this three-step process:

Step 1: Review your schedule. Ask yourself when you *must* check your email. Be honest. Be practical. Remind yourself that avoiding email for a few hours won't result in a catastrophe.

Step 2: Pick two times of the day. After tracking your energy levels for two weeks (see *Tactic #18: Manage Your Energy Levels*), you should have a good idea regarding how your energy fluctuates throughout the day. Pick two low-energy times of the day to check your email.

Step 3: Tell others about your new email policy. Your boss, coworkers, friends, and family members likely have certain expectations with regard to how long it takes you to respond to their emails. Let them know that going forward, you'll check your email twice a day. Inform them of the times of the day you selected in Step 2. Doing so will encourage them to shift their expectations (see *Tactic #16: Reset Others' Expectations*).

The purpose in checking your email twice per day is that it allows you to work with maximum focus. And importantly, it helps you to leverage those periods of the day when your energy levels are at their highest point.

If you're addicted to email, adopting this new policy may be difficult. Give yourself time to get accustomed to it. Also, give yourself a routine reality check. Whenever you're tempted to retrieve your email when you should be focusing on something else, ask yourself:

 "What's the worst that can happen if I avoid email for a few hours?"

You'll find that the worst possible scenario is highly unlikely, and thus not a valid concern.

TACTIC #21: CREATE (AND STICK TO) A DAILY ROUTINE

~

As much as we want to think of ourselves as spontaneous, most of us thrive on routine. The brain prefers structure. It likes to know what comes next. This allows it to focus on the next action rather than being distracted by a plethora of *potential* next actions.

This is the number one reason highly-productive people follow daily routines. They're able to devote more cognitive resources to tasks that require their attention. They can thus work more efficiently, and ultimately get more things done.

They don't need to worry about whether they have the motivation to act. Nor do they need to be concerned about whether they have enough willpower. Their routines prompt them to take action.

Think about your own daily patterns. You follow them, even if you don't realize it. For most people, these patterns are executed inside short periods of time. Consequently, most folks miss out on the increased focus that longer, more comprehensive routines offer.

For example, you probably go through the following ritual when you wake up in the morning:

- Brush your teeth
- Use the bathroom
- Take a shower
- Blow dry your hair
- Put on deodorant
- Apply makeup (for the ladies)
- Get dressed
- Eat breakfast

As you execute this series of actions, you don't need to think about what comes next. You've been going through the same routine for years. Each action, along with the overall order, has been ingrained in your mind through repetition. As a result, you can complete the entire routine efficiently without being distracted from it. You're subconsciously focused on each action.

You can leverage this same attentional quirk of your subconscious to effect a state of hyperfocus during your workday. Simply create a daily routine that prompts you to take action on recurring tasks. For example, suppose you need to do the following each day:

- Check email
- Return phone calls
- Create three daily reports for your boss
- Meet with your coworkers to discuss projects

And of course, you have a number of other tasks on your to-do list that need to be addressed at some point.

A hypothetical daily routine might look like the following:

- 8:00 a.m. - Arrive at the office

- 8:00 a.m. - 8:30 a.m. - Review your to-do list and pending projects. Add high-priority items to your list as necessary.
- 8:30 a.m. - 9:30 a.m. - Work on daily reports.
- 9:30 a.m. - 9:45 a.m. - Take a break.
- 9:45 a.m. - 11:00 a.m. - Work on daily reports.
- 11:00 a.m. - 11:20 a.m. - Meet with coworkers to discuss projects.
- 11:20 a.m. - 12:00 p.m. - Complete daily reports.
- 12:00 p.m. - 1:00 p.m. - Take lunch. Check and respond to email.
- 1:00 p.m. - 1:30 p.m. - Return phone calls.
- 1:30 p.m. - 2:15 p.m. - Work on tasks that require minimal energy (refer to your to-do list).
- 2:15 p.m. - 2:30 p.m. - Take a break.
- 2:30 p.m. - 3:30 p.m. - Work on tasks that require minimal energy.
- 3:30 p.m. - 3:45 p.m. - Meet with your boss about the following day's priorities.
- 3:45 p.m. - 4:00 p.m. - Take a break.
- 4:00 p.m. - 5:00 p.m. - Work on tasks that require medium-level energy.
- 5:00 p.m. - 5:15 p.m. - Check and respond to emails.
- 5:15 p.m. - 5:30 p.m. - Review the day's accomplishments. Create a to-do list for the following day.
- 5:30 p.m. - 5:40 p.m. - Clear off your workstation.

Notice that the above routine is a form of time chunking. You're assigning time chunks to address recurring items, such as email, phone calls, and reports. You're also designating periods to take breaks, lunch, and work through your to-do list.

Over time and with repetition, this pattern will become

deeply-rooted in your consciousness. Your brain will learn to expect what comes next.

As a result, you'll find it much easier to manage your attention. You'll be less prone to distraction, and able to stay on task when doing so is important.

TACTIC #22: TAME YOUR INNER PERFECTIONIST

~

I n the chapter *Top 10 Obstacles To Staying Focused*, I noted that interruptions cripple our ability to concentrate. I reiterated this point in *Tactic #16: Reset Others' Expectations.* There, we discussed interruptions in the context of other people imposing them upon us. Coworkers, friends, and family members disrupt our work, break our concentration, and take us out of a flow state.

It's worth addressing interruptions we impose upon *ourselves.*

Tell me if this sounds familiar...

You're writing an article, working on a report, or responding to an involved email. Along the way, you stop yourself repeatedly to research details, validate data, or edit what you've written. Each stop is a disruption to your workflow. Each one interrupts you and breaks your focus.

This is a problem commonly experienced by perfectionists. They're unable to proceed with the task at hand unless their work is of the highest quality. Unfortunately, their perfectionism prevents them from ever mastering their attention and getting things done.

I used to face this problem myself, particularly when writing. Every sentence had to be perfectly worded before I could move on to the next sentence. Oftentimes, I'd stop in the middle of a paragraph and go back to the preceding one to make edits. It was difficult to concentrate because I kept interrupting myself.

I eventually learned to tame my inner perfectionist and cease the self-imposed interruptions. Today, I write without stopping to make edits, confident that I'll do a much better editing job after the first draft has been completed. As a result, I'm able to focus more easily, and can do so for much longer periods.

I guarantee that taming *your* inner perfectionist will have the same effect. If perfectionism regularly spurs you to interrupt yourself, try the following:

Step 1

Work in 10-minute time chunks without correcting mistakes or making edits. Doing so will train your mind to work without interrupting yourself, even when you leave glaring mistakes in your wake.

Fair warning: it'll be difficult at first. Your inner perfectionist will protest. But rest assured, it'll become easier the more you do it.

Step 2

If you need to look up a particular detail or piece of data, simply jot down "XYZ" on whatever you're working on. Don't stop to find the information you need. Keep working. You can fill in the blanks later.

Step 3

Review your work after each 10-minute session. Fix the mistakes and add the necessary details.

You'll find that this approach is much more efficient than constantly interrupting yourself as you work. It streamlines your workflow, making it easier for you to get into the zone. Consequently, you'll find that you're better able to focus and ignore distractions.

To be sure, your inner perfectionist has good intentions. It wants you to do your highest-quality work. The problem is, it obsesses over this goal. It encourages you to interrupt your workflow over and over, thereby preventing you from building any significant momentum.

Tame your inner perfectionist to improve your ability to concentrate. You'll ultimately get more done and turn in better-quality work in less time.

TACTIC #23: REDUCE YOUR CAFFEINE INTAKE

$\sim$

First, the good news.

There are definitely benefits to consuming moderate amounts of caffeine. Studies show that doing so can increase your energy,[1] improve your memory,[2] and lift your mood.[3] Caffeine can even elevate your mental alertness.[4]

The problem is, many people consume too much caffeine. The consequences can be severe. They include persistent insomnia, restlessness, an increase in stress levels, and elevated blood pressure. Research has also shown that excess caffeine consumption can set the stage for anxiety disorders.[5]

It's clear the amount of caffeine we consume each day influences our ability to concentrate. Unfortunately, many of us mistake being *awake* with hyperfocus. We wrongly figure that as long as we're awake, we must be doing something right, and consequently consume more caffeine than is healthy. You may remember feeling jittery in the past after drinking too much coffee. Do you recall how difficult it was to concentrate?

Clearly, being awake isn't the same as being in a state of focus.

The key is to keep your daily consumption of caffeine to a moderate amount. Health experts claim that amount is approximately 400 milligrams. As a gauge, a 20-ounce cup of Starbucks "Pike Place" coffee contains 415 mg. A 20-ounce Caffè Americano, which comes with four espresso shots, contains 300 mg.

If you're drinking more than that, there's a good chance you're impairing your ability to concentrate. Consider cutting back. Doing so will not only help you to relax and enjoy better sleep, but it'll also help you to better manage your attention.

Unless your doctor suggests otherwise, there's no need to quit caffeine altogether. Again, moderate consumption delivers useful benefits. But if you're like millions of people who drink several cups of coffee each day, it's time to make a healthy change.

I speak from experience. I used to consume nearly 1,000 mg of caffeine each day. To say I was addicted would be an understatement.

Back then, I was sleeping four hours per night. I mistakenly thought I was handling things well because the caffeine kept me awake. And worse, I wrongly inferred that getting by on minimal sleep day after day was a sign of solid productivity.

In truth, I was an absolute mess. I lacked focus and had difficulty concentrating on even the simplest of tasks. I'd read a few pages in a book or magazine and be unable to recall what I had just read. Holding a conversation with me was like talking to a heroin addict. I was constantly distracted.

The culprit was the excess caffeine. Once I cut back, I was able to regain my focus. It was a long, frustrating process - that's the case with quitting *any* addiction - but I'm glad I made the effort.

Take it from me. If you're consuming too much caffeine on a daily basis, you're doing yourself a disservice. Reduce your intake and enjoy the resulting boost in mental clarity and concentration.

Fair warning: cutting back on caffeine is going to be difficult at first, especially if you're addicted to the stuff. After all, your brain has gotten used to enjoying a certain amount each day. Rest assured that over time, your brain will acclimate to the reduced level. The upside is that it's much easier to focus when you're not wired.

---

1. https://www.ncbi.nlm.nih.gov/pubmed/20888549
2. http://www.nature.com/neuro/journal/v17/n2/full/nn.3623.html
3. https://www.ncbi.nlm.nih.gov/books/NBK209050/
4. http://onlinelibrary.wiley.com/doi/10.2903/j.efsa.2011.2054/epdf
5. https://www.cambridge.org/core/journals/advances-in-psychiatric-treatment/article/neuropsychiatric-effects-of-caffeine/7C884B2106D772F02DA114C1B75D4EBF

PART IV

BONUS MATERIAL: HOW TO FOCUS WHEN WORKING IN COFFEE SHOPS

∿

More people than ever are trying to get stuff done in places like Starbucks, Gloria Jean's Coffee, Peet's Coffee, and Tim Hortons. They take their laptops to these venues and stake out tables (preferably near an outlet to keep their laptops charged) for hours on end.

You've seen them. In fact, you may *be* one of them. They work on reports, catch up on email, and prepare presentations. They schedule meetings, input data into spreadsheets, and crunch numbers. If they're teachers, you'll often see them grading papers.

These road warriors are working hard to get things done. They're valiantly trying to boost their productivity. But if you look closely, you'll notice that most of them are distracted.

They have their phones near them, and regularly interrupt their work to read and send texts and emails (or worse, play with their apps). Many of them look up whenever someone new walks into the venue. You'll also notice that most of these road warriors know other customers. These customers walk up to their tables to chat, and in doing so interrupt their concentration.

If you do any type of work in a coffee shop, I'm certain you can relate to the above. And you know intuitively how such interruptions can ruin your focus and destroy your momentum.

In the following (short) sections, I'll give you a quick, simple plan for maintaining your focus when you work in places like Starbucks. Put these suggestions to use, and you'll find it much easier to stay on task.

FACE THE WALL

~

I t's natural to want to have the wall at your back when
sitting in a coffee shop. That's the only way you'll be able to
see other people.

But that's precisely the problem. Facing the main area, you
have full view of everything. That presents a major temptation to
people-watch. The more people who walk in and out of the coffee
shop, the more tempted you'll be to look up from your work.

Worse, the temptation grows as the minutes pass. Staying
focused will become increasingly difficult as your brain tires and
begins to crave the distraction of external stimuli.

I recommend that you face the wall. Keep your back to the
main area of the coffee shop. The view will be less engaging, but
that's the point. With little to look at but your laptop and the wall,
you'll be less distracted.

It's akin to putting on blinders. By facing the wall, you limit
the external stimuli that can break your concentration.

You won't always be able to do this, of course. Seating will be
constrained by the venue's space limitations. If it's crowded, you

may be forced to sit near windows, giving you full view of outside scenery that can easily commandeer your attention. Or the coffee shop may be so crowded that you have no choice but to sit at a table located in the center of the lobby. People milling about the area can easily distract you.

Do the best you can. If necessary, set up at a table in a less-than-optimal location, and watch for tables to become available near walls. Relocate when one opens up.

IGNORE THE DOOR

～

There's something irresistible about looking to see who's entering a coffeehouse. Do you know the person? How old is he or she? What is the individual wearing? How do they hold themselves? What can you infer about their vocation? Are they regulars or new to the venue?

Most of us love to people-watch. It's part of our internal wiring. We can sit contentedly for long periods and do nothing more than observe others.

The problem is, this tendency can severely impede our ability to focus and stay on task. We interrupt ourselves every time we look towards the door. Each interruption breaks our concentration and forces our brains to spend valuable time getting back on track.

The solution is simple: ignore the door.

Admittedly, it's easier said than done. Looking up whenever you hear the door open may be a deeply-rooted habit. You may not even realize you're doing it. Breaking the habit will take time and patience.

Start small. Commit to five minutes without looking up from your work. Open a browser tab to Google and type "timer 5 minutes" (assuming the coffee shop offers Wi-Fi). Then, force yourself to work without lifting your eyes until the timer's alarm goes off.

Once you're able to work for five minutes without looking towards the door, set the timer for 10 minutes. Then, 15 minutes, Then, 20 minutes.

The length of time you force yourself to ignore the door is less important than the consistency with which you do it - at least in the beginning. The goal is to replace the bad habit with a positive one, using a slow, methodical process that makes it easier to retrain your brain.

I struggled with this bad habit years ago. Writing in Starbucks, I'd immediately look at the door every time someone walked in. I was like one of Pavlov's dogs. Consequently, it was nearly impossible to focus and stay on task.

Today, I rarely look at the door when I'm working in a coffee shop. My brain has been trained to ignore it. The upside is that it's much easier to concentrate for longer periods.

WEAR HEADPHONES (OR EARBUDS)

~

Headphones create a personal island of isolation. They indicate to other people that you're listening to music, a podcast, an audiobook, or some other type of media, and prefer not to be disturbed. When others see you wearing headphones, they take the hint and are disinclined to interrupt you.

On the other hand, without them, you're fair game. People are likely to approach you as you work.

Remember, we're social animals. We enjoy interacting with others, particularly those whom we know, like, and trust.

We're also curious by nature. When we see something that's unfamiliar to us, we're inclined to investigate. Don't be surprised when you're approached by strangers inquiring about the nature of your work. I've lost count of the number of times people have approached my table at Starbucks to ask (or state) the following:

- "Are you a teacher/professor?"
- "What do you do for a living?"

- "I see you in here every day. What kind of work do you do?"
- "How much time do you spend in this place? They should charge you rent!"
- "How much coffee do you drink each day?"

People want to interact, which is fine if you're taking a short break. But it can wreak havoc with your focus if you're trying to work.

Wearing headphones (or earbuds) solves this problem. It makes people less likely to barge in on you. Most will leave you to your work.

A few people will be persistent. They'll see your headphones and still decide to interrupt you.

Here's a tactic for addressing these interruptions that I've found to be very effective: I look the person in the eyes, give them a friendly (and slightly apologetic) smile, and say "*I'm sorry. I can't hear you with the music playing.*"

This gives the individual two options. He or she can be considerate and leave you to your work. Or he or she can ask you to pause the music, remove your headphones, and give them your attention.

You'll find that nearly everyone will choose the former option. A few may choose the latter, essentially ignoring your need and right to privacy. Personally, I have no problem refusing them my attention.

Over time, you'll find that the number of people who interrupt you will dwindle. You'll have reset their expectations.

By the way, you don't actually have to listen to music, podcasts, or audiobooks for this to be effective. The mere presence of headphones (or earbuds) will suffice.

LISTEN TO INSTRUMENTAL MUSIC ON A LOOP

∾

We covered the use of music in *Tactic #8: Play Music That Helps You To Enter A Flow State*. It's worth revisiting in the context of working in places like Starbucks, Peet's Coffee, and Tim Hortons.

For some, the normal bustle of activity in a coffeehouse offers the perfect backdrop to achieve a flow state. The noise of the espresso machine, the clamor of porcelain and silverware, and the general din of customers' banter help them to concentrate. This is the reason apps like Coffitivity[1] exist: to replicate the experience.

Personally, I've found music - specifically, classical piano pieces - to be more effective. This is especially true when the pieces are recorded in loops that play over and over. I can drown out the environmental noise and more easily focus on the task in front of me.

I mentioned earlier that I usually write while listening to a repeating track of Chopin's Prelude in E minor, Op. 28, No. 4. I also mentioned that you can find the following pieces recorded in 60-minute loops on YouTube:

- Beethoven's Für Elise
- Beethoven's Moonlight Sonata
- Chopin's Nocturne Op. 9, No. 2
- Erik Satie's Gnossienne No. 1
- Franz Liszt's La campanella

Give them a try. The next time you work in a Starbucks or any other coffeehouse, visit YouTube and search for the above pieces. Add the words "60 minutes" to each search query to find the tracks that have been recorded in hour-long loops.

If you're like me, you'll find that your brain will become so accustomed to the repeating music that you're able to easily focus and reach a flow state.

---

1. coffitivity.com

TRAIN OTHERS TO NOT INTERRUPT YOU

~

A s I noted in the section *Wear Headphones (Or Earbuds)*, most of us are social animals who enjoy interacting with others. Doing so gives us joy. Sharing a smile and exchanging a few friendly comments, even with strangers, fills us with a unique sense of satisfaction.

It's no wonder so many people are inclined to interrupt those of us who are working. They mean no harm. On the contrary, they're prompted by a sense of camaraderie and shared community.

Many coffee shops have the same vibe as bars and taverns. The people who frequent them are usually in an affable mood - at least, once they've had their first sip of coffee - and are inclined to engage those around them.

Given these circumstances, how can you minimize the interruptions without offending people? Here's a strategy that has worked for me:

When someone approaches my table, I refrain from looking up at him or her. I force that person to demand my attention.

Eventually, he or she will do so, attempting to start a conversation by asking a question or making a friendly comment.

I'll usually smile and offer a friendly, but succinct response, and then return to my work. If the person asks another question or makes another comment, I'll offer another friendly, terse response. Most people will get the hint and suspend their attempts to spark a conversation at this point.

If the individual persists, I'll smile and say *"I'd love to talk, but I'm under pressure to get this done."*

This statement is friendly and non-confrontational (smiling helps), and communicates that I'm trying to focus. It also underscores without saying so outright that the individual is preventing me from doing so.

The payoff comes later. When this person sees me working next time, he or she will be less inclined to interrupt me. The individual will assume that I'm trying to get things done, and thus need to concentrate.

This strategy's effectiveness isn't immediate. Resetting others' expectations takes time. But rest assured, it pays dividends over the long run. Folks will gradually become accustomed to not interrupting you when they see you, giving you the opportunity to focus and stay on task.

FINAL THOUGHTS ON DEVELOPING FAST FOCUS

❧

We've covered a lot of material in this action guide. The most important takeaway is that you're in control. When it comes to developing razor-sharp focus that allows you to fight distractions and stay on task, you have the necessary tools. It's just a matter of putting them to use.

I used to be one of the least focused individuals you'd have ever expected to meet. Today, I can zone in on whatever work is in front of me and easily ignore everything else.

It didn't come easy. And it didn't happen overnight. But realize that if I was able to do it, *you* most certainly can, too.

The upside is that you'll produce higher-quality work, make fewer mistakes, and get more done in less time. This in turn will allow you to spend more free time with the people you love and the hobbies and passions that excite you!

DID YOU ENJOY READING FAST FOCUS?

～

First, I'd like to thank you for reading this book through to its end. As you can tell, I'm passionate about this topic. I firmly believe that attention management is one of the keys to living a rewarding, productive life.

If you enjoyed reading *Fast Focus*, would you do me a quick favor? Would you leave a review on Amazon, telling others how the ideas in the book helped you to sharpen your focus?

Your review doesn't have to be long. A couple of sentences would be fantastic!

Your review will allow me to continue writing books that help people achieve measurable results in their lives. It'll also encourage others who want to learn how to master their attention to give *Fast Focus* a try.

I intend to publish several more time management and productivity action guides over the next year. Each one will contain actionable advice you can put to use immediately. Each one will be launched at a steep discount for a limited time.

If you'd like to be notified when I publish these books, be sure to join my mailing list at the following link:

http://artofproductivity.com/free-gift/

Notice the URL contains the words "free gift." When you join my mailing list, you'll receive my 40-page Special Report *Catapult Your Productivity: The Top 10 Habits You Must Develop To Get More Things Done*. It's in PDF format so you'll be able to read it on your computer, phone, or tablet. It's my way of saying "Welcome aboard."

You'll also receive my best tips, tricks, and hacks for managing your time, increasing your daily productivity, and designing a more rewarding lifestyle.

Thanks again for taking the time to read *Fast Focus*. Join my mailing list and stay in touch!

All the best,

Damon Zahariades
http://artofproductivity.com

ABOUT THE AUTHOR

Damon Zahariades is a corporate refugee who endured years of unnecessary meetings, drive-by chats with coworkers, and a distraction-laden work environment before striking out on his own. Today, in addition to being the author of a growing catalog of time management and productivity books, he's the showrunner for the productivity blog ArtofProductivity.com.

In his spare time, he shows off his copywriting chops by powering the content marketing campaigns used by today's growing businesses to attract customers.

Damon lives in Southern California with his beautiful, supportive wife and their frisky dog Rocky. He's currently staring down the barrel of his 50th birthday.

OTHER BOOKS BY DAMON ZAHARIADES

The Mental Toughness Handbook

The definitive, step-by-step guide to developing mental toughness! Exercises included!

To-Do List Formula

Finally! Discover how to create to-do lists that work!

The Art Of Saying NO

Are you fed up with people taking you for granted? Learn how to set boundaries, stand your ground, and inspire others' respect in the process!

The Procrastination Cure

Discover how to take quick action, make fast decisions, and finally overcome your inner procrastinator!

How to Make Better Decisions

Here's how to overcome indecision, make smart choices, and create a rewarding life in the process!

The 30-Day Productivity Plan

Need a daily action plan to boost your productivity? This 30-day guide is the solution to your time management woes!

The 30-Day Productivity Plan - VOLUME II

30 MORE bad habits that are sabotaging your time management - and

how to overcome them one day at a time!

The Time Chunking Method

It's one of the most popular time management strategies used today. Triple your productivity with this easy 10-step system.

80/20 Your Life!

Achieve more, create more, and enjoy more success. How to get more done with less effort and change your life in the process!

Small Habits Revolution

Change your habits to transform your life. Use this simple, effective strategy for adopting any new habit you desire!

Morning Makeover

Imagine waking up excited, energized, and full of self-confidence. Here's how to create morning routines that lead to explosive success!

The Joy Of Imperfection

Finally beat perfectionism, silence your inner critic, and overcome your fear of failure!

The P.R.I.M.E.R. Goal Setting Method

An elegant 6-step system for achieving extraordinary results in every area of your life!

Digital Detox

Disconnect to reconnect. Discover how to unplug and enjoy a more mindful, meaningful, and rewarding life!

For a complete list, please visit

http://artofproductivity.com/my-books/